W9-BQV-382

# SHIPWRECKS AROUND CAPE COD

## (Illustrated)

### by William P. Quinn

A collection of photographs and data covering the period
from the late 1800's to 1973 on Cape Cod.

One of the most distressing occupational hazards of fishing is when the boat sinks. A Provincetown fishing boat sprung a leak in the middle of the night. The next morning she rests on the bottom of the harbor and the crew have many extra days of work before they can go fishing again. *Photo by Neil Nickerson.*

*COPYRIGHT,© 1973, BY WILLIAM P. QUINN*

*All rights reserved.*

*Library of Congress Catalog Card Number: 73-92326*

ISBN 0-936972-01-7

*Printed in the United States of America by*
The Knowlton & McLeary Co.
Farmington, Maine

*FIRST EDITION REVISED*

*Seventh Printing*

*Published by:*

Lower Cape Publishing
P.O. Box 901
Orleans, Mass. 02653

# PREFACE

For longer than anyone alive today can remember, ships have been wrecked on the backside of Cape Cod. I can remember as a boy, growing up on the backside in the 1930's, we used to sleep on the outer beach in the deck house of the wrecked schooner *MONTCLAIR* during the summertime.

This book is a collection of photographs that began over 20 years ago. Some of the pictures are spotted and scratched, some are from old broken glass plates, faded and dusty from the years of storage. Some were copied from old photographs loaned by friends. Not all of the reproductions are perfectly sharp and clear.

During the collecting of the photographs and data, research is long and sometimes unsuccessful. Most of the stories are checked twice where possible but sometimes the items gleaned from newspapers and marine publications are not always reliable. An old schooner Captain once said that the worst scoundrels made the best seamen. These men with dubious pasts were sometimes the survivors that reported the facts in the events surrounding a shipwreck and they could stretch the truth from Highland Light to Peaked Hill Bars.

Most of the factual information came from the men who lived it. Old timers who can remember the storms and fogs, the wrecks and survivors. They spun the yarns and I became fascinated in the wonder of their impossible rescues and how they accomplished what they did with the crude apparatus of the life savers of that time.

Most sea stories have a touch of romance interwoven with the plot but there is little glamour in disasters. How these men performed their duties in the face of overwhelming odds is the exciting part of life saving. The romance and glamour is written between the lines of the record books.

W.P.Q.

Wreckers salvage rigging from the remains of the *F/V FORTUNA* after it washed up on the beach at Race Point, Provincetown. The vessel was wrecked on February 12, 1894.

*This book is dedicated with much love*
*and many thanks to my mother*
**EVA L. E. QUINN**
*whose assistance and keen memory*
*helped to complete this book.*

The wreck sits on the beach and the waves eat away at the hull and the sand works around the ribs as the winds drive another two masted coaster off shore on the port tack off Peaked Hill Bars, Provincetown. *Photo courtesy of Cape Cod Photos, Orleans.*

# CONTENTS

**1** The early years before photographs. The first Cape Cod Shipwreck. The *SOMERSET* and the *FRANCES* . . . . . . . . . . . . . . . . . . . . . . . . . . . . . . . . . . . . . . . 7

**2** Building a wall of ships along the back shore of Cape Cod. Sailing vessels wrecked and an early view of the Life Savers of Cape Cod. . . . . . . . . . . . . . . . . . . . . . . . . . . 23

**3** 19th Century commerce on Cape Cod. The Mooncussers, the Wreckers and beach-combers. The fog wrecks, the Portland gale and the Monomoy Disaster. . . . . . . . . . . . . 45

**4** The Iron Ships. As the steamer replaced the sailing ship, the iron ships began to appear on the beaches of Cape Cod. . . . . . . . . . . . . . . . . . . . . . . . . . . . . . . . . . . 69

**5** Wrecks around the Islands. Down through the years the storms and fogs of Nantucket and Martha's Vineyard have taken a heavy toll of ships. . . . . . . . . . . . . . . . . . . 81

**6** The history, construction and opening of the Cape Cod Canal at the beginning of the 20th century. Some early wrecks in the canal with modern photographs of the waterway. . . . . . . . . . . . . . . . . . . . . . . . . . . . . . . . . . . . . . . . . . . . . . . . . . . . . 93

**7** World War One and the German Sub attack on Cape Cod in 1918. The Rum Runners and the Submarine disasters on the Cape during the roaring 20's. . . . . . . . . . . . 111

**8** The last sailing ship wreck on the backside of Cape Cod and an interview with one survivor. The quiet 30's with few wrecks on Cape Cod. . . . . . . . . . . . . . . . . . . . . . . . 129

**9** The blocking of the Cape Cod Canal during World War Two, Torpedo junction, the *VINEYARD LIGHTSHIP* and the *CAPE ANN*. . . . . . . . . . . . . . . . . . . . . . . . . . . . 141

**10** Drama on the high seas off Cape Cod when two oil tankers split in half at the same time. Another ship aground at Peaked Hill Bars. . . . . . . . . . . . . . . . . . . . . . . . . . 149

**11** "There's another wreck at the canal." Shipwrecks occur in the waterway under all conditions fair and foul and from sulphur to gypsum. . . . . . . . . . . . . . . . . . . . . . . . . 161

**12** Collision at Sea . . . . The memorable disaster of the *ANDREA DORIA* and the *STOCKHOLM* in 1956 and the *HORNBEAM* in 1972. . . . . . . . . . . . . . . . . . . . . . . 181

**13** The Coast Guard Today on Cape Cod and surrounding waters. Modern equipment speeds rescues in the jet age. . . . . . . . . . . . . . . . . . . . . . . . . . . . . . . . . . . . . . . . . 189

**14** The storms of the 50's and 60's strand the fishing boats, the ships and even the Coast Guard and others. . . . . . . . . . . . . . . . . . . . . . . . . . . . . . . . . . . . . . . . . . . 209

**15** Winding up a Century of photographs of shipwrecks on outer Cape Cod. . . . . . . . . . . . . 223

The reproductions of the charts in this book are courtesy of the National Ocean Survey, N.O.A.A., U.S. Department of Commerce and are not for navigational use.

Cape Cod and the Islands as seen from high above the earth aboard Skylab II in June of 1973. The Astronauts got a mapmakers view of the southern New England shoreline. *Photo courtesy of the National Aeronautics and Space Administration.*

# CHAPTER 1

**The early years before photographs.
The first Cape Cod Shipwreck.
The *SOMERSET* and the *FRANCES*.**

In Shakespeare's "Tempest" the scene is on a ship at sea, a storm, with thunder and lightning and an old counsellor of Naples named Gonzalo says "Now would I give a thousand furlongs of sea for an acre of barren ground." Gonzalo could be speaking for hundreds of men in similar circumstances all over the world. On Cape Cod, northeast storms, ocean fogs and even a misread compass have brought disaster to sailors and ships passing this dangerous shoreline. Eighteenth century pirates, East Indiamen, Coasters, Gloucester fishermen and Whalers have spread their spars up and down the backside of Cape Cod.

In 1626 the first such mishap occured on Nauset Beach in what is now Orleans, when the small vessel *SPARROWHAWK* foundered on the shore in a northeast storm. It has been over 300 years since that first recorded shipwreck on the outer shores of the Cape and thousands have followed. Today, on a dune buggy trip down Nauset Beach in Orleans and Chatham you can still see evidence of by-gone wrecks. The sun bleached bones of schooners and square riggers of another era are there buried in the dunes.

It was not uncommon that scores of ships were wrecked on the sands of the Cape to lie and rot. The equipment of navigation in the early days of sailing left much to be desired, by today's standards, when a storm was in the making. The Mariner had a compass, a leadline, a barometer and a chart. There were some lighthouses and buoys but no other aids were available and, in good weather, none were needed. However, when the barometer began to drop, and the tell-tale clouds started to make up in the western sky, the sailors had to shorten sail and batten down the hatches for stiff weather ahead.

Author Henry C. Kittredge had some interesting comments about shipwrecks in his book: "Cape Cod — Its People & Their History" (1930)

"It has been said that if all the wrecks which have been piled upon the back-side of Cape Cod were placed bow to stern, they would make a continuous wall from Chatham to Provincetown. This is a picturesque way of putting what is substantially the truth, for Peaked Hill Bars and the Monomoy Shoals are to sailors today what Scylla and Charybdis were to Æneas. Nauset Beach, which stretches along the whole coast line of Orleans and Eastham, holds in its fatal sands the shattered skeletons of vessels from half the seaports of the world; while farther north, the outer shores of Wellfleet and Truro have gathered in the hulls of a thousand ships, driven helplessly upon them by northeast gales."

Ships are no longer piled up on the backside of Cape Cod with the same frequency as in the old days. Improved methods of navigation have all but eliminated the disasters. Occasionally a fishing boat will come aground inside the outer beach surf and become another statistic, but radio beams and Loran navigation have aided in keeping the ships out of the deadly

The three masted schooner *MAUDE BRIGGS* wrecked Dec. 31, 1901 at the Nauset Station in Eastham. Offshore a four masted schooner plies her way north. A very beautiful but common sight in those days. *Photo by H. K. Cummings, Orleans.*

area just off Cape Cod. Advance weather bureau warnings on bad storms, ship to shore telephones, radar, fathometers and reliable power for vessels have battled Mother Nature to the point where, with the coming of the Cape Cod Canal, the shipwrecks on the outer shore began to wane, until today wrecks occur only once every two or three years. One hundred years ago, wrecks occurred on an average of once every two or three weeks. A bad storm might cast two or three ships up on the outer shores of the backside. These wrecks, in the 1870's, meant work for the wreckers and the economy of the Cape prospered. A wreck in the 1970's brings large crowds of tourists to view the sight and to take pictures, spending money, so the economy still prospers.

If you were unfortunate enough to be shipwrecked on Cape Cod before 1870, your chances of survival were not very good. Any aid for the shipwrecked sailor had to be a matter of luck, as the only ones along the barren shoreline in winter were the beachcombers and wreckers. If you lived through the ordeal of the wreck, there was no comfort on the shore, as you would have to walk for miles to find any shelter from the elements.

The Massachusetts Humane Society was formed in 1786 by the Rev. James Freeman, the Parson of the King's Chapel in Boston. Soon after organization, the society began to move

8

The British schooner *JOHN S. PARKER* from St. John, N.B. to New York City with a cargo of lumber was wrecked in Nauset Inlet on Nov. 7, 1901 at 2:30 A.M. The Life Savers landed six men via the breeches buoy and although the schooner was a total loss, part of the cargo was saved. *Photo by H. K. Cummings. Orleans.*

towards the relief of the sailor cast ashore. The society began to build small, closed sheds along the shores and called them charity houses. First aid kits, canned foods, a fireplace with fuel and flares were among the items contained in the charity houses to aid the shipwrecked sailors. The first was built in 1807 in Boston Harbor on Lovell's Island. The Commonwealth of Massachusetts and the Federal Government made contributions to the society to help defray the costs of the houses along the coasts.

The method of rescuing people by breeches buoy was originated in 1791 by a Lieut. Bell of the British Royal Artillery using a mortar to fire a line-carrying projectile to a ship in trouble on the shore. Down through the years, countless thousands have been saved using the breeches buoy apparatus. The last time the breeches buoy was used to save men from a stranded ship was in Provincetown on January 16, 1962 when the fishing vessel *MARGARET ROSE* stranded on New Beach early in the morning. Since then the apparatus has been retired out of the Coast Guard service and is no longer used. Modern methods have replaced most of the ancient equipment. Amphibious vehicles, motor lifeboats and helicopters have replaced the old hand rowed lifeboat and the breeches buoy. The charity houses have long since fallen into dust and some of the Coast Guard stations along the shoreline have become private homes, while others have been torn down.

ABOVE: The British Brig *MATILDA BUCK*, from Gonaives for Boston with a cargo of logwood, went ashore on Jan. 9, 1890 a half mile from Wood End Light. The crew were rescued by wreckers throwing a line on board and sending off a boat. *Photo courtesy of Cape Cod Photos. Orleans. Data from New York Maritime Register Jan. 15 & 22, 1890.*

OPPOSITE ABOVE: The Provincetown fishing vessel *VALERIE*, 139 tons, driven ashore during a winter gale in 1918. OPPOSITE BELOW: The Steamer *H. F. DIMOCK* aground on Nauset Beach in Orleans on March 10, 1909. *Photo Courtesy of Tales of Cape Cod. Barnstable, Mass.*

ABOVE: The Swedish Motor Vessel *MONICA SMITH* stranded on New Beach in Provincetown. The ship was riding out gale force winds off Provincetown on Feb. 21, 1960 when she grounded and ended up high and dry. *Photo by Quinn* .
BELOW: The 524 foot Norwegian Freighter *TAGAYTAY* went aground in the fog on a mud shoal off Sias Point in Cape Cod Canal by mis-reading the radar on Saturday Dec. 11, 1971. The vessel was carrying 2,000 tons of general cargo from New York City to Boston. The Corps of Engineers tug *MANAMET* had a line aboard the ship trying to pull it out of the mud. The ship was pulled free the next day and continued on her way to Boston. *Photo by Sumner Towne-Cape Cod Independent*

# THE FIRST SHIPWRECK ON CAPE COD

Early shipwreck data was included in the records of all Cape towns dating back to the 1700's. The type of ship, cargo, names of the Captain and crew and the deaths are painstakingly listed in longhand and some of the records are epic in description.

The earliest record of a shipwreck was written about 2,000 years ago and comes from the Bible. (Acts-Chapt. 27) St. Paul was cast ashore on the island of Malta and the ship he was on became a total wreck. The earliest record of shipwreck on Cape Cod was in mid-December 1626, a tiny vessel *SPARROWHAWK* foundered on the sands of Nauset Beach. The account of the wreck is found in Bradford's History. A small ship, with cargo and passengers bound from Plymouth, England to Jamestown, Virginia. The actual number of people aboard was not mentioned but the size of the *SPARROWHAWK* leaves little doubt, perhaps eighteen to twenty-three persons could squeeze aboard the small ship for a voyage across the Atlantic.

Running into foul weather off Cape Cod, the ship ended up on the beach and, meeting friendly Indians, the crew sought help from the Plymouth settlement. The ship was repaired and set back to sea again but only to fall again to the storms. The passengers and crew had to spend the winter in Plymouth while the elements and the shifting sands swallowed up the *SPARROWHAWK* into the marsh at Nauset after the local Indians had burned the upper part of the hull.

The first shipwreck on Cape Cod. The skeleton was removed from Nauset Beach after a storm uncovered the remains in 1863. Presently on display in Pilgrim Hall in Plymouth, Mass. *Photo by Quinn.*

In 1863, a storm uncovered the remains of the ancient vessel and the skeleton was removed from the sands and re-assembled into a display. The *SPARROWHAWK*'s bones were shown around New England, Boston Common, Providence, Rhode Island and ended up in Plymouth, Massachusetts at the Pilgrim Museum, where they are now housed along with many other articles of Pilgrim memorabilia.

It is an inherent trait of modern historians to question the authenticity of relics, and the remains of the *SPARROWHAWK* are no exception, however the type of construction has checked with early records of ships of that era and so the conclusion is that no one can prove that the remains are not those so indicated.

The weather was not the only contributing factor in this early disaster. When you translate Bradford's History into modern day language, it seems that after a voyage of many weeks across the Atlantic, the *SPARROWHAWK*'s supplies were running low. The water casks were empty and "they had drank all their beer." The concensus was to seek out the first available land. The Captain was sick with scurvy, so conditions aboard the small vessel were not quite shipshape. The *SPARROWHAWK* came ashore at night and shortly thereafter the passengers met up with Indians. There have been many accounts written on the *SPARROWHAWK* adventure, most are interpretations of the facts from Bradford's History.

OPPOSITE: Model of the *SPARROWHAWK. Photo courtesy of Peabody Museum of Salem.* BELOW: Original Draught of *H.M.S. SOMERSET*, 64 gun frigate built 1748 in Chatham, England, wrecked on Peaked Hill Bars, Provincetown, November 2, 1778. *Draught from National Maritime Museum, London, England.*

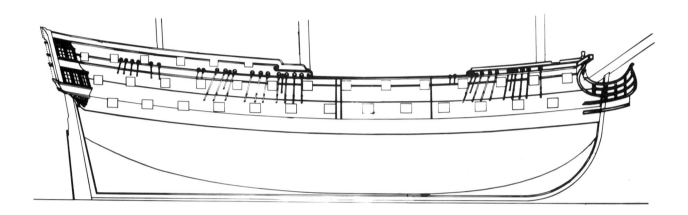

One of the more notable wrecks, in the early days, was that of the British Man-o-War *SOMERSET*. During the Revolutionary War, the wreck of the *SOMERSET* brought joy to the hearts of Cape Codders when she met her fate on Peaked Hill Bars, November 2, 1778.

The *SOMERSET* was a third rate frigate built in Chatham, England and launched July 18, 1748. She was 64 guns and drew duty in the colonies for most of her career. The *SOMERSET* covered the landing of British troops for the battle of Bunker Hill in Charlestown, Massachusetts and was prominent in Longfellow's poem about Paul Revere's ride. In the third verse of the famous poem, Henry Wadsworth Longfellow (1807-1882) wrote:

> Just as the moon rose over the bay,
> Where swinging wide at her moorings lay
> The Somerset, British Man-o-War;
> A phantom ship, with each mast and spar,
> Across the moon like a prison bar,
> And a huge black hulk, that was magnified
> By its own reflection in the tide.

The *SOMERSET* was a frequent visitor to Provincetown Harbor, and while there the Captain made himself unwelcome when he sent provisioning parties ashore to appropriate fresh supplies for his ship at no cost. Instead of paying for the provisions, Captain George Curry sent his Chaplain ashore on Sundays to preach to the good people of Provincetown. There can be little doubt as to the contents of the sermons.

Cape Cod was entirely unprotected during the Revolutionary War and the English had complete control over the waters around the Cape. During this time there were minor skirmishes and it was during one of these that the *SOMERSET*, in pursuit of some French Merchant ships, ran into a storm off Cape Cod and tried to make it back around Race Point and into Provincetown Harbor. The huge frigate failed to clear Peaked Hill Bars and the storm did extensive damage to the ship when she hit on November 2, 1778. About 50 crewmen drowned while trying to reach shore during the height of the storm.

The *SOMERSET*. British Man-o-War, a 64 gun ship leading Lord Howes fleet sailing from Sandy Hook, July 1777. *Photo courtesy of Mariners Museum, Newport News, Va.*

The Cape Cod Militia assembled and captured Capt. Curry and his remaining crewmen and marched them to Boston under guard where they were put in prison. The wreck of the *SOMERSET* was supposed to be a prize of the Colonies, but most of the prizes went to the industrious Cape Codders who got there first. Everything of any value was recovered by the Cape wreckers. The cannon were removed and shipped to Boston for coastal fortifications. Cape Codders completed payment for the debt that had been partially paid in preaching and prayers.

After most things of value were removed from the wrecked frigate, some of the zealous patriots burned the hull. The flames only consumed the upper part of the ship while the lower portion was sanded in to the dunes and remained for many years buried at Peaked Hill. For the next hundred years the remains were in and out of the sands and what was left became smaller as years went by. The huge oak timbers that were her lower hull section were cut away, little by little, and became ship models and other items of remembrance from the ship. The bones of the *SOMERSET* came out of the sands again at Peaked Hill Bars in June of 1973 and caused a heavy influx of viewers and history buffs.

ABOVE: Remains of the British Frigate *SOMERSET* on Peaked Hill Bars in Provincetown. Ship wrecked on Nov. 2, 1778 in Northeast Gale, picture taken in 1886 when the bones washed out of the sands. *Photo courtesy of Cape Cod Photos, Orleans, Mass.* RIGHT: Marking on beam of *SOMERSET* Roman numeral XXII. *Photo by Quinn.* BELOW: The bones of the English Frigate *SOMERSET* on Peaked Hill Bars. Photo taken on June 21, 1973. *Photo By Quinn.*

This is an artist's conception of the trauma of a shipwreck. This photo is a reproduction of an old English print of a sailing ship on the rocks with life savers trying to rescue the people on board. *From a print courtesy of William Carter of Dover, Mass.*

Photographs of the earliest shipwrecks do not exist. From the first shipwreck in 1626 down to the mid-1800's when the photographs started to appear, paintings and drawings from an artist's conception were the only visual depictions that men had to see the wrecks.

In the early 1800's there were many disasters including a monster storm in 1841 that made many widows from Newfoundland to Delaware. Hundreds of fishing vessels were wrecked at sea and the survivors were picked up clinging to wreckage all over the North Atlantic.

From the "Report of Ship Canal" published in 1864, in the interest of the construction of a canal from Cape Cod Bay to Buzzards Bay, a table of shipwrecks shows that from 1843 to 1859 there were over 800 shipwrecks on Cape Cod. Not all were total wrecks and not all involved loss of life, but the statistics were clear and concise. In those days, most coastal commerce was moved by ships. In 1849, early historians reported that 16,000 vessels sailed east around Cape Cod while another report states that in 1875, approximately 15,000 vessels passed Chatham Lighthouse.

The basic raw materials for shipwrecks were plentiful in this area. In a sense that was unfortunate because the outer Cape shoreline, along with Cape Hatteras in North Carolina, is described as the most dangerous coastline for shipping in the United States. Cape Cod has an appalling record of shipwrecks. The tidal currents are shifting constantly as are the shoals and invisible sand bars that reach out to snag ships and draw them into a watery grave. Gales occasionally reach hurricane force of 70 MPH or better, and dense fog sometimes blinds the mariner seeking port. All of these natural hazards were aided and abetted by human errors when crewmen would mistake a land light for a lightship or lose their bearings and go aground in the surf.

Aerial photograph of the remains of The Hamburg Bark *FRANCES* just off shore at Head of the Meadow Beach, within the Cape Cod National Seashore in Truro. *Aerial photo by Quinn.*

In 1871, Congress gave birth to the Lifesaving Service. The act establishing the service passed and the stations were built along the coastal areas to relieve the growing number of deaths attributed to shipwrecks.

On the stormy night of December 26, 1872 the Hamburg Bark *FRANCES,* Capt. Wilhelm Kortling, Master, from Passaroeang, Batavia and Singapore, bound for Boston with a cargo of sugar and tin, was wrecked on shore one mile from Highland Light at nine o'clock, Thursday. The vessel was badly iced up from the northeast gale blowing at the time of the wreck.

Capt. Worthen, newly appointed keeper of the Highland life saving station, went to the aid of the vessel and crew. The *FRANCES* was a three masted iron hulled bark with a crew of 14 men. She was 120 feet long and, shortly after she struck, was a total wreck. With volunteers, Capt. Worthen went to the Massachusetts Humane Society station across the Cape on the Bay side, and with much difficulty the volunteers dragged and skidded the boat across the Cape to the outer beach and launched it in the raging surf to go out and rescue the 14 men on the ship. The crew of the *FRANCES* was exhausted from their battle with the elements, but all were landed by the Lifesavers and Capt. Worthen.

Capt. Wilhelm Kortling had been sick for three weeks prior to being shipwrecked on the Cape. He died in Provincetown three days later and was buried in the cemetery in Truro. The remains of this wreck are still visible at low tide in Truro at Head of the Meadow Beach. The hull was in and out of the sands for almost 100 years. For the past few years has been out at the beach in Truro.

LEFT: Capt. Kortling was buried in Truro. There are many graves like this throughout the lower Cape. Some are not identified as names of many shipwrecked seamen were never known. *Photo by Quinn.* CENTER: Chart 1208 shows the wreck of the *FRANCES* on the backside of the Cape between the Highlands L.S. station and the High Head Station. BOTTOM: The broken remains of the Hamburg Bark *FRANCES* wrecked December 26, 1872. The iron hull has lasted over 100 years at the Highland area, Truro. *Photo by Quinn.*

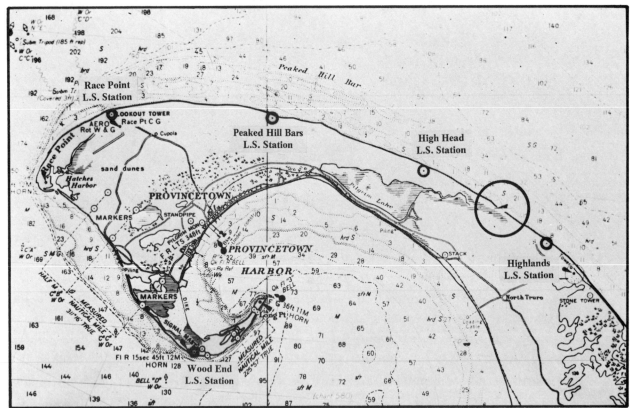

ABOVE: The Maine fishing schooner *ELLEN LINCOLN* was wrecked on December 31, 1895 three miles north of the Nauset Station in Eastham. The crew of 19 was saved by the Lifesavers but the vessel was a total loss. BELOW: The British schooner *LILY* ashore at Eastham on Jan. 3, 1901. A cargo shift 15 miles at sea caused the schooner to leak seriously while her mainsail and outer jib were torn to shreds and her skipper headed for the beach. Lifesavers tried to help but before they could launch their boat the crew of the *LILY* came ashore in their own boat. The *LILY* was a total loss and went to pieces in the heavy surf. *Photos by Henry K. Cummings, Orleans.*

The schooner *PLYMOUTH ROCK* aground on Peaked Hill Bars in Provincetown on April 11, 1888. Loaded with lumber the *PLYMOUTH ROCK* came ashore in the same spot that, two years earlier, the three masted schooner *HANNAH E. SHUBERT* met her fate. The bones of the *SHUBERT* can be seen in the foreground of the photograph. *Photo by Rosenthal, courtesy of Cape Cod Photos.*

# CHAPTER 2

**Building a wall of ships along the back shore of Cape Cod.**
**Sailing vessels wrecked and an early view of the Life Savers of**
**Cape Cod.**

In 1839, Louis Jacques Mandé Daguerre made the first practical reproductions on metal plates and called them daguerreotypes. Later a German named Voigtländer improved Daguerre's invention and with a new type of lens introduced photography to the world.

It wasn't until 1870 that new and faster plates were produced and photography became instantaneous. At this period, pictures of shipwrecks began to appear, and many spectacular photographs were made of the disasters.

In 1888 George Eastman introduced roll film and the Kodak Camera became a universal instrument for all. Subsequent developments in the photographic field have created an art form very near perfection.

On March 9, 1886, a lifesaver from the Peaked Hill Bars station on patrol found a three masted schooner aground on the outer bar, about 500 yards off shore and a mile east of the station. The lifesaver burned a coston signal and went back to the station to bring help. They launched a surfboat and boarded the stricken vessel. The *HANNAH E. SHUBERT,* 398 tons from Perth Amboy, N.J. to Boston, Mass., with a cargo of coal was stuck hard on the bar and efforts by the lifesavers to free her were futile. They ran out a kedge anchor and tried to heave her off the bar, but while the work was in progress, a heavy northeast squall came up and the salvage attempt had to be abandoned. On the next flood tide the vessel swept over the shoals and stranded upon the beach where she became a total wreck. A portion of the cargo, the anchors and sails were saved by a party of Provincetown wreckers.

Three master schooner *HANNAH E. SHUBERT* ashore at Peaked Hill Bars, Provincetown, March 1886. *Photo courtesy of Cape Cod Photos, Orleans, Mass.*

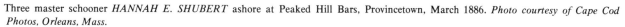

ABOVE: Ship *A. G. ROPES* damaged in a squall off Nantucket on July 12, 1888. 19 yards and spars carried away in the storm. Capt. Rivers jury-rigged her and brought her into Provincetown Harbor for repairs and re-rigging on July 21, 1888. LEFT: Men re-rigging ship *A. G. ROPES* in Provincetown Harbor, August 1888. OPPOSITE: Ship *A. G. ROPES*, Capt. Rivers, leaving Provincetown Saturday, Sept. 29, 1888 under full sail, without tug assistance, proceeding on voyage to San Francisco where she arrived on Thursday Jan. 17, 1889, 110 days out of Provincetown. *Photos courtesy of Cape Cod Photos, Orleans.*

At 4 A.M., April 11, 1888 the patrol from the High Head station reported a light at the eastern end of Peaked Hill Bars and a vessel ashore. The keeper of the High Head station manned the surf boat and went to the vessel. The weather at the time was developing into a southeast gale with heavy surf rolling. When they reached the ship they found that seas were already breaking over her and she was breaking up. The *PLYMOUTH ROCK* of Boston, Mass., bound from St. John, N.B., to New York City with a cargo of lumber. The ship came ashore one hour after midnight when she overestimated her distance from shore.

The crew of six was landed in the surf boat all suffering from exposure and then taken to the High Head station for relief. On a succeeding tide the vessel pounded over the outer bar and came upon the beach where she went to pieces. Henry Kittredge said "they would make a continuous wall from Chatham to Provincetown" this ship came ashore at the exact spot that two years earlier the *HANNAH E. SHUBERT* was lost. The photograph shows the bones of the *SHUBERT* protruding up through the sands with the *PLYMOUTH ROCK* in the background.

Three months later the *A. G. ROPES*, flagship of the I. F. Chapman Company of New York was passing by Nantucket bound for San Francisco with a cargo of oil products when she ran into a violent squall and lost 19 yards and spars from her rigging. Under a jury rig she was worked into Provincetown Harbor, which Capt. Rivers chose as a port of refuge, rather than return to New York for fear that his crew might jump ship there, after having been paid a large sum in advance money to ship for the voyage. Advance money was discontinued in the 1890's by the U.S. Shipping Commission.

Provincetown ship builder John G. Whitcomb was engaged with his riggers to assist Capt. Rivers and his crew of 35 to re-fit the ship with new spars and yards, sails and rigging, all brought from Boston, Mass., and Bath, Maine in the Packet Steamer *LONGFELLOW*. The story of the wreck of the *LONGFELLOW* appears later in the section on steamers.

The *A. G. ROPES* was considered the finest example of post-clipper, fast sailing, cargo carriers, and known as the "Great Down Easters". Built for global shipping, California trade, the Orient and Frisco to Great Britain. Fastest passages "Frisco to Britain" in 104 days.

Her 21 yards ranged from 7″ to 21″ in diameter. In August, 1905 sailing from Hong Kong to Baltimore she was again dismasted in a South China Sea typhoon. Capt. David Rivers again jury-rigged her and sailed her into New York, arriving in May, 1906, where she was sold to the Lewis Luckenbach Transportation Company for conversion into a coal barge.

She was lost with a crew of five men in a New England storm off Forked River, New Jersey on December 26, 1913, while in tow of the tug *EDGAR F. LUCKENBACH* en route from Delaware Breakwater to Providence, R.I. filled with coal.

Early in the morning of February 16, 1890 a patrol from the Nauset Lifesaving station in Eastham discovered the four masted schooner *KATIE J. BARRETT* aground 350 yards from shore at the southerly end of the beach at Nauset Inlet. The surfman burned his coston signal and returned to the station to bring help.

The crew of the Nauset Station rowed through heavy surf to board the schooner. Nothing could be done at the time as the tide was dropping and the vessel was hard aground. The vessel was out of Boothbay for Philadelphia, of 963 tons with a cargo of ice and a crew of nine. Later that day the lifesavers landed the crew and the ship was left to the wreckers.

The ship stayed on the bar for three days with wreckers trying to float her off with each tide. Every time the tide was high enough for the ship to float, she seemed to edge nearer to shore until on the 19th she was driven over the outer bar and on the beach high and dry.

The condition of the ship continued to deteriorate until the following September when wreckers floated her on a high course tide and tugs towed the hull to Boston. However the rudder and many other small implements off the vessel stayed on Cape Cod. There are many homes in the Eastham and Orleans area with marine memorabilia nailed to the walls of dens and playrooms along with these same photographs of the wreck. The wheel of the *KATIE J. BARRETT* was for many years a lawn ornament in Orleans.

RIGHT: Orleans inlet changes with every tide. The *KATIE J. BARRETT* came ashore between two Lifesaving Stations. (Chart 1208) BELOW: Deck view of *KATIE J. BARRETT* aground at Nauset Inlet with wreckers aboard and lighter alongside, Feb. 25, 1890. *Photo by H.K. Cummings, Orleans.* OPPOSITE: The four masted schooner *KATIE J. BARRETT* aground in Eastham/Orleans at Nauset Inlet, Feb. 24, 1890. *Photo by H. K. Cummings, Orleans.*

For the seven months that the hull of the *KATIE J. BARRETT* lay on the sands at Nauset Beach. Photographer Henry K. Cummings made repeated trips to the scene. He recorded the gradual deterioration of the ship. A study in contrast as the masts came down and she was striped of her gear.

Travel of the day was limited to horse and wagon (see photo, pg. 28 - bottom) and along with heavy camera equipment, it made a difficult pull for the horse through the beach sand.

Probably the most important factor in the ultimate salvage of this hull was the constantly shifting sand bars at Nauset Inlet. The tide run here has a heavy scouring action on the bottom and the salvagers were lucky enough to pull her off at just the right time.

The *KATIE J. BARRETT* aground at Nauset Inlet with a cargo of ice from Maine, with a lighter alongside. *This photo printed from a broken and scratched plate. Photo by H. K. Cummings, Orleans.*

This is the condition of the hull before it was refloated in September 1890. The three year old vessel is badly hogged. *Photo by H. K. Cummings, Orleans, Mass.*

28

In March 1890 the *KATIE J. BARRETT* is losing her fight with the elements and her masts are coming down. The hull is still intact here even though she is sanded in and the surf hits her with every tide. BELOW: This photograph taken March 22, 1890 shows the *KATIE J. BARRETT* awash in the surf with her masts gone and water breaking over her decks. An interesting feature of the photo is that it shows the beginning of the end of the sailing era. Just off shore you can spot an auxiliary steamer on the horizon and another hull down beyond her. *Photos by Henry K. Cummings, Orleans, Mass.*

RIGHT: Insignia of the U.S. Life Saving Service. OPPOSITE: Launching a Jersey type surf boat, U.S.L.S.S. *Photo from the collection of Paul C. Morris, Nantucket, Mass.* BELOW: From the Highland Station, a Monomoy type surf boat. *Photo by Small, courtesy of the Bourne Historical Society.*

The United States Life Saving Service was created in 1871 by the Congress in an effort to cut down on fatalities from shipwrecks along the coastline of the United States. The Coast Guard as we know it today did not come into being until January 28, 1915 when the two services were merged into one. The Revenue Cutter Service and the Life Saving Service became the U.S. Coast Guard, and both worked together with one common purpose, "To protect life and property from the ravages of the sea."

Up to this time, both services enjoyed enviable records in their respective fields. The Revenue Service was originated by Alexander Hamilton in 1790 as the Revenue Marine to enforce the country's law on the high seas. Winter cruises began in 1831 giving aid to persons in distress at sea, preserving property and saving cargoes of wrecked vessels.

The Life Saving operations on the shoreline began in 1786 when the Massachusetts Humane Society was formed. Much later, the work of the organization was recognized by the Congress who appropriated money to aid in the continuation of the relief of the shipwrecked mariner.

ABOVE: The Race Point Life Savers in a surfboat drill. Constant practice kept lifeboat crews sharp and experienced. The seasoned man had a better chance of living when the going got tough and "you had to go out". *Photo courtesy of Cape Cod Photos, Orleans.* OPPOSITE TOP: Crew of the Orleans Station. (circa 1899) L. to R. Orien Higgins, Mathew Kingman, Nehemiah Hopkins, John Hopkins, Edward Kendrick, Abbott H. Walker and Capt. James Charles. *Photo by H. K. Cummings.* OPPOSITE CENTER: The Orleans Life Saving Station at the turn of the century housing men, beach apparatus lifeboat and a horse. *Photo courtesy of Harry Snow, Orleans.* OPPOSITE BOTTOM: Life Saving crew of the Orleans Station with the beach cart apparatus in a drill. The Breeches Buoy apparatus was towed to the scene of the wreck by the horse then the men went to work. Not very fast but efficient. *Photo by H. K. Cummings, Orleans*

It wasn't until 1850 that the Federal Government decided to build their own lifeboat stations. In that year, Congress appropriated $10,000 to build and equip the stations but provided no funds for personnel. The stations and shipwrecked sailors depended on volunteers to carry out the vital work. The early stations were small buildings housing a surfboat and other material of the day to be used in saving lives.

In 1854, Keepers were appointed for the stations at an annual salary of $200 and in 1871 Congress authorized funds to hire surfmen to man all of the Government stations. The first station was built at Spermacetti Cove in Sandy Hook, New Jersey and this small building has been preserved and is now a Coast Guard Museum.

The museum contains some of the first surfboats used in ship rescues, the breeches buoy apparatus with the Lyle guns used to fire a line carrying projectile to a wreck. Some pieces of early shipwrecks and some old logbooks containing the first entries of shipwrecks and disasters at the beginning of the Life Saving Service.

It has been over 100 years now since these efforts were begun. The records reveal impressive figures — over 200,000 lives and over two billion dollars in property have been saved by the cutters and lifeboat stations.

In the beginning the pay was $40. a month, the food was edible but the work was dangerous. The Rule book said "You have to go out"; it made no reference to coming back. Most of

them did come back though and wrote epic chapters into the record books of life saving and devotion to duty. Those first years of the Life Saving Service were recorded in J. W. Dalton's book "The Life Savers of Cape Cod" published in 1902 just after the Monomoy Disaster, and reprinted in 1967. It is a detailed account of the men of the service stationed on Cape Cod and stories of the more historic disasters around the outer Cape beaches.

The record books of the U.S. Life Saving Service are filled with exciting tales of rescues and shipwrecks. The 1884 edition of the Annual Report told of an incident involving a Cape Cod Lifesaver who single handedly saved the entire crew of a vessel aground on the backside of the Cape.

"On April 3, 1884 at 2 A.M. the weather was rainy and dark with a strong northeast wind blowing and a rough sea. Surfman F. H. Daniels, of the Cahoon's Hollow Station (in Wellfleet) on the south leg of his patrol saw a bright light ahead which was a distress signal from the schooner *VIKING*. He at once started on a run and in a short time arrived abreast of a schooner aground in the breakers about 50 yards from the beach near Newcomb's Hollow, two miles north of his station.

"His first thought was to keep on and alarm his comrades, but upon considering the time it would take to get to the station he determined on a bold effort to save the vessel's crew single handed. The bright light that had attracted his attention was still burning when he arrived. It was clothing saturated with kerosene the crew had lighted for a signal for aid.

OPPOSITE:   Orleans Life Savers setting up apparatus for Breeches Buoy Drill. Circa 1900. *Photo by Henry K. Cummings, Orleans.*

ABOVE: Surfboat returning to shore. Life Saving Service. *From the collection of Paul C. Morris, Nantucket.*

The whole scene was brilliantly illuminated by it, and the sailors, seeing Daniels arrive, watched their opportunity and threw him the end of a lead line. This he managed to secure by rushing down into the surf, and in a few minutes the end of a larger line was bent to it and drawn ashore. One of the men then secured the bight of the rope around his body, and, with a shout to Daniels to haul away, plunged into the boiling surf. The gallant surfman was equal to the task, and, with the water waist-deep around him, he pulled on the rope and succeeded in landing the man all right, and the latter exclaiming, as he staggered to his feet upon reaching the beach, "For God's sake, who are you." The reply of Daniels was brief and to the point: "I am a life-saving man, and you must lend me a hand to save the rest." At a signal from Daniels the line was quickly hauled back, and in a short time the entire crew, twelve in all were safely landed, those last rescued narrowly escaping injury from the floating wreckage of two dories which had been smashed to pieces alongside the schooner in an attempt to launch them soon after the vessel struck. It was about 3 o'clock when the last man was drawn ashore and then Daniels, after turning the water out of his hip boots, started with the wrecked crew for the station.

"The men reported their schooner as the *VIKING,* of Gloucester, Massachusetts, on her way from the Georges Bank, with a fare of fish for Boston. The schooner and cargo were lost, nothing but the sails and rigging being saved. Her crew remained at the station until the following day, when they were sent home to Gloucester by rail at the expense of the Wellfleet Benevolent Society. The men upon leaving, expressed much gratitude to the station crew, and especially to Surfman Daniels, to whom they acknowledged they owed their lives." 35

ABOVE: The Race Point Life Saving Station. One of the first built on Cape Cod was cramped for space. BELOW: One of the first improvements made by the Life Saving Service at the turn of the Century was to update their stations. This was the later type of building at Wood End, Provincetown. The larger station afforded more roomy quarters for the men and was preferred over the smaller structures. *Photos courtesy of Cape Cod Photos, Orleans.*

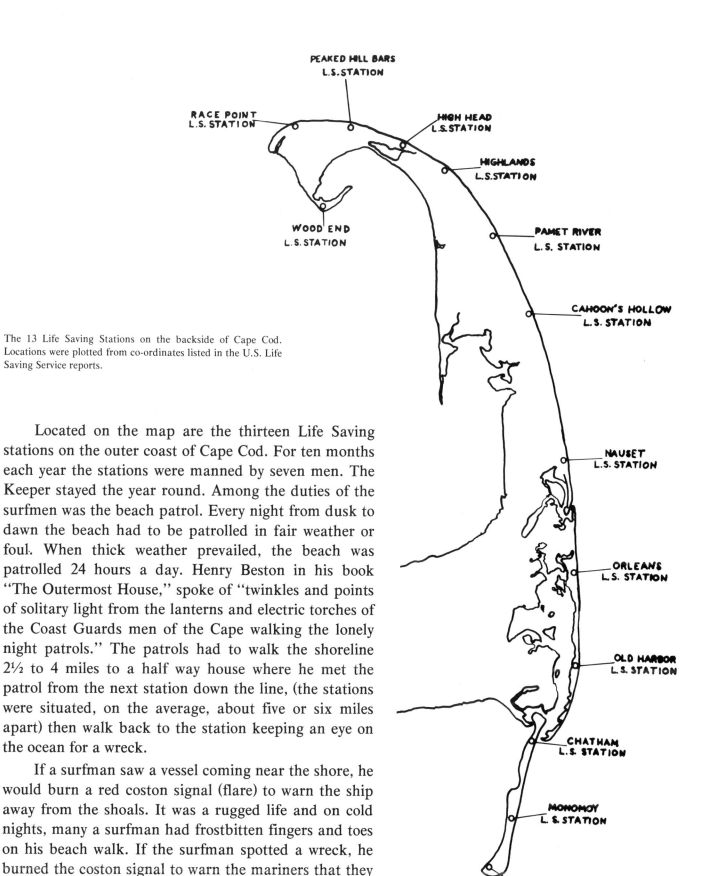

The 13 Life Saving Stations on the backside of Cape Cod. Locations were plotted from co-ordinates listed in the U.S. Life Saving Service reports.

Located on the map are the thirteen Life Saving stations on the outer coast of Cape Cod. For ten months each year the stations were manned by seven men. The Keeper stayed the year round. Among the duties of the surfmen was the beach patrol. Every night from dusk to dawn the beach had to be patrolled in fair weather or foul. When thick weather prevailed, the beach was patrolled 24 hours a day. Henry Beston in his book "The Outermost House," spoke of "twinkles and points of solitary light from the lanterns and electric torches of the Coast Guards men of the Cape walking the lonely night patrols." The patrols had to walk the shoreline 2½ to 4 miles to a half way house where he met the patrol from the next station down the line, (the stations were situated, on the average, about five or six miles apart) then walk back to the station keeping an eye on the ocean for a wreck.

If a surfman saw a vessel coming near the shore, he would burn a red coston signal (flare) to warn the ship away from the shoals. It was a rugged life and on cold nights, many a surfman had frostbitten fingers and toes on his beach walk. If the surfman spotted a wreck, he burned the coston signal to warn the mariners that they had been seen, and help was on its way. He then hurried to the station to awaken the crew to go to the aid of the stricken vessel.

There were two courses of action for the Keeper of the station. The first was to bring the beach apparatus to the scene, fire a line to the vessel and set up the breeches buoy to bring in the shipwrecked sailors. If the vessel lay too far off shore, then the life savers would try to launch a surfboat into the raging seas to go out to bring in the imperiled men. The seas were usually raging, as northeast storms were the breeders of disasters along the coast and weather conditions were always at their worst when the Life Saving crews had to go out.

37

ABOVE: The British Bark *KATE HARDING* ashore on the backside in Truro. She hit with such force that it tore the bottom out of her. Wreckers are shown five days later stripping the bark of sails and cargo. BELOW: View of the stern of the British Bark *KATE HARDING* on the beach at Truro. The British sailors are standing on the beach at the stern of the vessel while the long white mass hanging down from the after part of the ship is a sail all bundled up for salvage. More sails can be seen on the beach beside the vessel. Date of the photograph is Dec. 5, 1892. The Ship does not appear in this photo to be badly damaged but the damage was on the bottom of the vessel. *Photos by H. K. Cummings, Orleans.*

38

The *KATE HARDING*. A later photograph taken before she was broken up by wreckers. Although of British registry, this vessel, as are many pictured in this book, was part of the Canadian Maritime fleet. *From the collection of Paul C. Morris, Nantucket, Mass.*

A prime example of the damage done during a northeaster, happened on the night of November 30, 1892. A dangerous sea was running and the British Bark *KATE HARDING* hit the outer bar off North Truro with such force that the ship was damaged beyond repair.

Life Saving crews from the Highland and High Head stations worked together to land the crew of ten men from the ill fated bark by the breeches bouy. The *KATE HARDING* was 712 tons and was commanded by Captain Wellington Perry. The quarterboard from this vessel is on display at Truro in the Historical Association building near Highland Lighthouse.

The introduction of the U.S. Life Saving Service report for the fiscal year ending June 30, 1894 cites, "The most disastrous wreck that has occurred within the scope of the service operations in recent years was that of the British Ship *JASON* on the 5th of December 1893 near the Pamet River station (Second District) coast of Cape Cod, Massachusetts."

The *JASON* was a full rigged ship out of Greenock, Scotland. 1,512 tons with Captain McMillan, bound from Calcutta, India to Boston, Massachusetts with a cargo of 10,000 bales of jute and a crew of 24 men. Thick weather prevailed off the coast for several days preceeding the disaster and the Captain was unable to determine his position. He obtained his whereabouts from a New York pilot boat on the 3rd of December.

While about 100 miles off the coast after passing Georges Banks, he unfortunately shaped his course to the westward for the purpose of raising some landmark. When the *JASON* approached the Cape, the wind was blowing a gale, from the northeast, and the atmosphere was thick with rain which, with the falling temperature, soon turned to sleet and snow.

The *JASON* was last seen before five in the afternoon by the day patrol of the Nauset Station out in thick weather as normal procedure. Information about the ship was telephoned along the line of stations up the backside of the Cape. At all stations from Nauset to Race Point, the horses were hitched to the beach carts and all preparations were made to go to the aid of the ship should it be required.

Shortly after 7 p.m. the *JASON* struck the outer bar, about a mile north of the Pamet River station. "The shore was almost immediately piled high with wreckage, and the slatting of the sails of the wrecked ship sounded like peals of thunder above the roar of the surf." A careful lookout for the shipwrecked sailors was kept along the shore by the Life Savers, and then the sole survivor of the disaster was found.

Samuel J. Evans was found clinging to a bale of jute, clad in only his underwear and suffering from exposure. He was rushed to the station and wrapped in warm blankets and he recovered soon after. The Life Savers then turned to try to save any other possible survivors and they fired a shot line over the craft which was dimly visible through the storm, but the entire crew, save one, had been lost as soon as the ship had struck and the efforts of the Life Savers were to no avail. The bodies of 20 of the crew were found and because of the reported overcrowding in the cemetery in Truro, they were buried in the cemetery vault in Wellfleet. Total loss of ship and cargo was listed in the records as $119,420.00.

Sometimes, shipwrecks begat shipwrecks. Abandoned schooners at sea were listed as derelicts, floating on the surface and a menace to other craft. A wooden hulled schooner hitting a derelict at night under moderate speed might become wrecked and sink with all hands.

40

OPPOSITE: THE REMAINS OF THE SHIP *JASON*. The vessel was wrecked in Truro, Dec. 5, 1893 with a loss of 24 lives and only one survivor. This photograph has been reproduced many times and is famous all over New England. It has been used extensively to depict a sailing shipwreck. *Photo by Henry K. Cummings.* RIGHT: Samuel J. Evans of Raglan, England, sole survivor of the wreck of the *JASON*. Evans was found by Lifesavers on the beach clinging to a bale of jute and lived to tell the tale of the disaster. In the background are bales of jute. *Photo courtesy of Tales of Cape Cod Inc., Barnstable.*

The Schooner *MESSENGER* was a derelict for a while. A three master sailing from Pensacola, Florida on October 23, 1894 with 240,000 feet of hard pine lumber as cargo. The ship stranded on the rocks opposite Peconic, Long Island on November 6, 1894 and was hauled off in a waterlogged condition after some of her deckload had been removed and taken to New London harbor. The schooner was taken in tow by the tug *ALERT* and at 5 a.m. on the morning of November 15th while fifteen miles northwest of Highland Light, the vessel capsized. The crew was rescued by the tug at the time.

After the ship capsized, the *ALERT* attempted to tow the derelict, but as her own pumps were choked with coal dust and water, she had to abandon the wreck and head for Boston. The *MESSENGER* was on her beam ends and abandoned when passed by the fishing schooner *VIKING\**, on November 24th, 18 miles off Thatchers Island, off the coast of Cape Ann on the north shore of Massachusetts. The *VIKING* made an effort to tow her in, but no headway could be made. She was in the track of passing vessels and was a dangerous obstruction to navigation.

She was washed ashore on November 26, 1894 at Cahoon's Hollow station in Wellfleet. On December 5, 1894 the *MESSENGER* was reported to be sanding in on the beach. The *MESSENGER* was 132 feet long with a 31 foot beam and was built in Bath, Maine in 1881, and her Captain was Charles Peters.

The *MESSENGER* was a loss to her owners. The ship had a long list of shareholders: Ellen M. Kelly - 30/64, Susie E. Carrington - 16/64, W.W. Burgess - 4/64, Albert H. Nute - 4/64, Jas. M. Simpson - 2/64, Harry L. Kelley - 2/64, Wm. Waters, Jr. - 2/64, Jas. W. Loveland - 1/64, Harry Loveland - 1/64 and the Master Charles Peters - 2/64.

1/64 share in a vessel does not sound like a huge amount but in those days it represented a goodly sum and its loss was not looked upon as a trifle. The majority of this list probably had a 1/64 share in many other vessels of that day so as to protect them against a heavy loss should one vessel be lost in a wreck.

*This is not the Schooner Viking referred to in Life Saving Rescue on page 35.

OPPOSITE — ABOVE: Wreck of the three masted schooner *MESSENGER*, ashore at Calhoon's Hollow in Wellfleet. Some wreckers on shore gathering wood from the wreckage. The *MESSENGER* was wrecked at sea and the derelict washed ashore Dec. 6, 1894. BELOW: On January 5, 1895, the schooner *JOB H. JACKSON, JR.* was wrecked near Peaked Hill Bars, Cape Cod during a gale. The vessel had lost her sails and had become unmanageable. Life Saving crews from the Peaked Hill Bars and High Head stations launched a boat in high seas and effected the rescue of the crew of nine. Some of the crew were badly frostbitten. The schooner was a total loss. *Photos by Henry K. Cummings, Orleans, Mass.*

ABOVE: The process of burial. Little by little the ocean moves the sand in and around to swallow up the hulls that sit in the surf and Mother Nature tries to return the beach to its natural state and bury the foreign objects. Many times a storm will alter the face of the beach and wash out wreckage of ships that have been buried for years. Then in time, cover them up again. *Photo courtesy of Cape Cod Photos, Orleans, Mass.*

ABOVE: Three coastal schooners tied up at the pier in Provincetown. Freight was big business on the sea before the big trucks took over on highways. *Photo courtesy of Cape Cod Photos* BELOW: Just after midnight on May 6, 1896, in a thick fog with a heavy sea running, the Newport, R.I. schooner DANIEL B. FEARING stranded about one mile north of the Cahoons Hollow Life Saving Station in Wellfleet. The Life Savers launched their boat and after a difficult pull, removed the crew of nine and brought them to safety. The heavy seas continued to pound the vessel and she broke up and was a total loss. The schooner was out of Philadelphia bound for Boston with a cargo of coal. *Photo courtesy of Capt. W.J.L. Parker, U.S.C.G. (Ret.)*

# CHAPTER 3

19th Century commerce on Cape Cod.
The Mooncussers, The Wreckers and The Beachcombers.
The fog wrecks, the Portland Gale and the Monomoy Disaster.

During the 19th century the sailing vessel carried on the commerce of the world. This continued into the 20th century until the steamships, with their dependable schedules and greater safety, stranded the square riggers and coastal schooners in deserted anchorages to rot away and die.

During this period, the sailing vessel was the most reliable mode of transportation for both goods and people. Highway stagecoaches were uncomfortable and unreliable at that time. They had to ford streams, fight off highwaymen and many times suffered breakdowns in the wilderness miles from any town.

On Cape Cod, fishing schooners, packet boats and square riggers were constantly plying between Cape ports and Boston, New Bedford and New York with trade goods. The majority of the people preferred to travel by packet boat. The sailing craft offered greater assurance for arrival at one's destination over the more dangerous land travel of the day.

The packet boats, small two masted schooner types, had limited accommodations for passengers, and the small space led to an equalization of the social distinctions. The prominent minister, squire or doctor had to book passage beside their less wealthy neighbors. This common ground had a tendency to lead to better understanding between the classes at that time.

There were most always, in the daytime, men on the beach for one purpose or another from the 18th century on down until today. Mooncussing was a term applied to the unlawful practice of luring ships to the shoals on dark nights with lanterns on the beach. Most of the alleged "Mooncussing" was supposed to have happened on Cape Hatteras on North Carolina. The town of Nags Head was named after the legend about pirates who tied a lantern around the neck of a horse. Then as the horse was led along the tops of the sand dunes, ship captains thought that the light was another ship anchored in a snug harbor. When they headed for the light they were wrecked on the treacherous shoals of the outer banks of North Carolina.

Some of the less exciting and more legal entrepreneurs were the wreckers and beachcombers. There was not too much difference between the two except that the wrecker was the more eager for profit and plied his trade with vigor. Whereas the beachcomber was content with whatever he found at his feet in the surf as he walked along the beach.

During these days of sail the ships were forever at the mercy of the elements and countless wrecks occurred on the backside of the Cape. When Congress voted funds to build lightships and erect lighthouses along the shores, the wreckers cries were heard all along the coast. They objected to the encroachment into their lifelihood. "It will ruin the economy" said one. The wrecks were a way of life and the men who made profit by the mariners misfortune saw no reason to change the odds in favor of the men who went to sea.

OPPOSITE TOP: The *CROSS RIP LIGHTSHIP* #5. Circa 1890. *Photo - Courtesy Louis Cataldo - Tales of Cape Cod - Barnstable.* OPPOSITE BELOW: *POLLOCK RIP LIGHTSHIP,* hull #73 before the turn of the century. *From the collection of Paul C. Morris, Nantucket, Mass.*

BELOW: The commerce in Provincetown before 1900 consisted of fishing. On the pier, fish drying on flakes while in the background the fleet lies at anchor. BOTTOM: A Bark getting ready to tie up at the pier at Provincetown with her crew furling the sails. *Photo courtesy of Cape Cod Photos, Orleans.*

ABOVE: The three sisters at Nauset in Eastham were the early warning lights for mariners. Circa 1890. These were replaced by a single lighthouse which stands there today. *Photo by H. K. Cummings, Orleans.* OPPOSITE: The Monomoy Lighthouse. Built in 1823 at the tip end of Monomoy Island (at the time) and rebuilt in 1855 and again in 1870. Discontinued use in 1923. The tower was painted red, 40′ high with a fixed white light containing a red sector which covered Pollock Rip Channel. The Island is now a wildlife refuge for shore birds. *Photo by Quinn.* BELOW: Billingsgate Lighthouse circa 1890. Lighthouse and island have disappeared, only the stone base of the lighthouse remains on the island and seen only at low tide. *Photo by Henry K. Cummings, Orleans.*

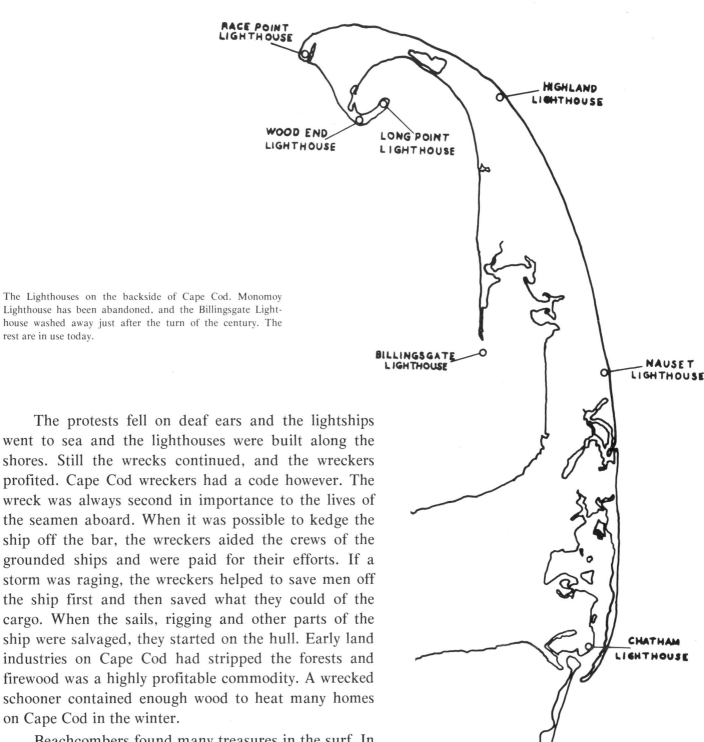

RACE POINT
LIGHTHOUSE

HIGHLAND
LIGHTHOUSE

WOOD END
LIGHTHOUSE

LONG POINT
LIGHTHOUSE

BILLINGSGATE
LIGHTHOUSE

NAUSET
LIGHTHOUSE

CHATHAM
LIGHTHOUSE

MONOMOY
LIGHTHOUSE

The Lighthouses on the backside of Cape Cod. Monomoy Lighthouse has been abandoned, and the Billingsgate Lighthouse washed away just after the turn of the century. The rest are in use today.

The protests fell on deaf ears and the lightships went to sea and the lighthouses were built along the shores. Still the wrecks continued, and the wreckers profited. Cape Cod wreckers had a code however. The wreck was always second in importance to the lives of the seamen aboard. When it was possible to kedge the ship off the bar, the wreckers aided the crews of the grounded ships and were paid for their efforts. If a storm was raging, the wreckers helped to save men off the ship first and then saved what they could of the cargo. When the sails, rigging and other parts of the ship were salvaged, they started on the hull. Early land industries on Cape Cod had stripped the forests and firewood was a highly profitable commodity. A wrecked schooner contained enough wood to heat many homes on Cape Cod in the winter.

Beachcombers found many treasures in the surf. In April of 1852 Freeman Mayo of Eastham was walking the beach when he discovered a broken mast from a shipwreck. Tied to the mast was a 12 year old lad still alive but quite cold. The boy was John Fulcher, cabin boy of the English Brig *MARGARET* which had been wrecked in a storm off Cape Cod. John lived in the Mayo home for a while then took up farming as his life's work. After his experience with the sea, John decided that the farm was a safer job. He married and settled in Eastham and was the progenitor of the now large Fulcher family of the outer Cape.

Many of the Editors of the weekly newspapers on the Cape are crusty charactors with salt water running through their veins and occasionally will relate some chin scratching prose of questionable truth about the early Cape people. The following essay was brought to light in a recent edition of the Cape Codder Newspaper in Orleans:

Wreckers waiting for the tide to go out at the wreck of the *JOHN S. PARKER*. Nauset Inlet, Nov. 1901. *Photo by H. K. Cummings, Orleans.*

# "SKULLDUGGERY ON THE SANDS"

It was, at best, a precarious profession. If the moon didn't rise you worked. If the moon rose, you loafed. The hours were terrible, the work dangerous and the returns dependent on too many tricks of fate. It was called Mooncussing and if it had one advantage as an occupation, it was the low overhead. All you needed was a lantern, a good supply of oil, and some supplementary equipment such as a slicker, sack and gaff. On the darkest nights of the year, you betook yourself to the nearest beach, lit the lantern and waved it in imitation of a ship swaying and tossing on the waves. If you were lucky, and some one else was not, a passing ship would take it for another vessel, follow the light and come to grief on the shore. Its cargo would be fair game as salvage.

If you had any tinge of conscience, you could probably rationalize that you were merely abetting the forces of nature. While not the oldest profession, Mooncussing was of a goodly vintage. It is said it started in England, on dry land, where "Moon Cursers" lighted the way for travelers right into the arms of confederates who robbed them. "Mooncussers" was a corruption of the original label and became known in this country particularly at Cape Hatteras, where the occupation was said to be followed with diligence and success.

Wreckers pick over the remains of the barge Pine Forest, one of three barges wrecked in a storm off Cape Cod on January 10, 1911. The wood salvaged from the wreckage was used mostly as firewood but some of the larger beams were used in construction of houses. *Photo courtesy of Tales of Cape Cod, Inc., Barnstable, Massachusetts.*

Business was understandably bad on moonlit nights. Hence the cursing of the moon as it mocked them from the sky. The question of whether Mooncussers existed on Cape Cod is almost certain to start a debate. Some people insist the Mooncussers are still here, running legitimate businesses, while others maintain the Cape's reputation was tarnished by the bad publicity from Cape Hatteras and other points along the Atlantic coast. It does seem that the Cape would be an ideal place for the trade. Miles and miles of unbroken lonely beach, a treacherous shifting sand bar, a well-traveled shipping lane. The stories are many and varied, and for the most part unsubstantiated. One story has it that Monomoy Island was the haunt of an incredibly evil white mare and a detestable old devil who practiced the trade. For fun. She had fire-red eyes and a soul blacker than the Stygian night. She was once the property of a clergyman, but had eaten too much cemetery grass. She became what is known as a fey horse, which means she knew ghosts, devils and other supernatural types.

On india-ink nights, when the wind howled in from the sea, her master would hang a lantern on her tail and make another fast to her mane. All night long, in the worst weather, she would patrol the beach, luring vessels into the shore. Then she and her master would snicker banefully. In later years, she would have been called a nightmare.

51

There is no one who can vouch the truth of this story, but Monomoy did have somewhat of an unsavory reputation. Once a shipwrecked sailor is said to have fought his way through the surf to shore. When told he had come to Monomoy, he turned and dived back into the raging sea, preferring to take on the more objective forces of nature.

Generally speaking, however, the first thought of the Cape Codder during a shipwreck was for the men, and often they risked and lost their lives attempting to save them. This was clearly evidenced by the early establishment of a life-saving system on the Outer Beach. It cannot be denied that a wreck did provide the Cape man with a harvest of treasure and articles of use still manage to melt mysteriously off the beach even now when a ship comes ashore. The Mooncusser label as applied to the Cape Codder, was probably a misnomer for the Wrecker, who did trudge the shore. Even this name is misleading because Wreckers were merely beachcombers, intent with only the jetsam and flotsam nature sent them. And it was no doubt fortunate, for many a ship in trouble, that these men were on the shore to see their plight. Cape Cod's best known publicist, Henry David Thoreau who was something of a beachcomber himself, encountered a number of Wreckers when he trekked the Outer Beach in 1859 and subsequent trips.

He talked with one whom he described as "a regular Cape man . . . with a bleached and weather beaten face, within whose wrinkles I distinguish no particular feature. It was like an old sail endowed with life, hanging cliffs of "leather-beaten flesh." He was looking for wrecks, old logs, water logged and covered with barnacles, or bits of boards and joists, even chips which he drew out of reach of the high tide and stacked up to dry. When the log was too large to carry far he cut it up where the last wave had left it, or rolling it a few feet, appropriated it by sticking two sticks into the ground crosswise above it."

Thoreau has passed on, but the beach is still there and so are the Wreckers. They still comb the beach for driftwood, exotic shells or anything else of interest but they do it more for fun than survival. And the Mooncussers? No one can say. But one way to find out would be to take a walk along the Outer Beach some night. If you come across a man mumbling "darn you moon", or even stronger invectives. Or you see a white mare sitting idly on her haunches, twiddling her hoofs and playing checkers with a detestable old devil who is complaining about the high cost of kerosene, you will have your answer.

# THE FOG WRECKS

"Damn the fog, head er off to wind'ard" . . . . . There is an old saying on the Cape that "over on Nantucket, they manufacture the fog and send it over here." Sometimes during the boiling hot days of summer, a cool ocean fog rolling in brings relief to the landsman but the fog is a greater enemy to ships than the northeast storms. Some of the more noted wrecks due to fog occurred on the Cape just before the turn of the century. On March 14, 1895 at 4 A.M. the 1,576 ton schooner *CHARLES A. CAMPBELL*, in ballast, stranded in the area of Pamet River station in Truro.

The Lifesavers went on board and found her aground in low surf and in no danger. They assisted at the sails, and remained by the vessel for six hours. They used their surfboats to run lines to tugs for two days while salvage attempts were going on. Lifesavers were well versed in sailing a schooner and sometimes had to stay with a ship into a New England port after aiding her when she was pulled off the Cape shores. Tugs pulled the *CAMPBELL* off the beach on March 16th and towed her into Provincetown. The Lifesaving crew stayed aboard the *CAMPBELL* at this time and accompanied her to Provincetown as they were unable to land at the time of the refloating because of high winds and surf.

OPPOSITE ABOVE: On March 14, 1895 the 1,576 ton schooner *CHARLES A. CAMPBELL* stranded in the area of Pamet River Station at 4 A.M. during thick foggy weather. The schooner was lying easily and in no danger as the surf was not dangerous at the time. Two days later the vessel was floated and towed to Provincetown Harbor by tugs. OPPOSITE BELOW: The four masted American Schooner *HAROLDINE* ashore in Eastham on November 8, 1895. The schooner became lost in the fog and ended up on the beach. She was refloated 12 hours later by a tug and continued her trip to Boston. *Photos by H. K. Cummings, Orleans.*

ABOVE: Two masted schooner ashore in the fog. The *ETHEL MAUD* stranded 1½ miles east of the Race Point Life Boat station at 2:45 A.M. on May 2, 1897. Life Savers rushed a boat to the scene but the schooner was high and dry when they arrived and the life savers walked aboard her. The 81 ton schooner was a total loss. Wreckers are removing the gear from the hull. *Photo courtesy of John Bell, Provincetown.*

The *CHARLES A. CAMPBELL* ran aground on Cape Cod again on October 7, 1912 when she hit the beach four miles south of the Cahoon's Hollow station in Wellfleet. Bound from Norfolk, Va. to Boston with a cargo of coal, she was again removed from the grounding without a loss.

On November 8, 1895 the American schooner *HAROLDINE* came ashore at Eastham at 3 A.M. in a dense fog. She was bound from Boston to Philadelphia under the command of Capt. Higgins. The patrol from the Nauset Station spotted the wreck and burned a coston signal. He then returned to the station to alert the crew. They brought a surfboat to the scene and boarded the vessel. The surf was moderate so no assistance was required of the Lifesaving crew. The Lifesavers did yeoman duty for the grounded vessel and telephoned for a tug. Twelve hours after the grounding the *HAROLDINE* was pulled free from the Cape sands.

A small two masted schooner stranded during a dense fog at 2:45 A.M. on May 2, 1897 in Provincetown. She was the *ETHEL MAUD*, 81 tons commanded by Captain Shehan. The ship came ashore 1½ miles east of the Race Point station and Lifesavers brought the surfboat to the scene but the schooner was high and dry when they arrived and the Lifesavers walked aboard her. The vessel was a total loss.

55

The 124 ton British Schooner *WALTER MILLER* stranded on Nauset Bar in Orleans on June 10, 1897 in dense fog. A heavy sea was running and life savers removed the crew of five and one woman by the breeches buoy. *Photo by H. K. Cummings, Orleans.*

The summer fogs of the Cape are as dangerous as the fogs of winter. On June 10, 1897 the 124 ton British schooner *WALTER MILLER* stranded on Nauset Bar in Orleans 2¼ miles north of the Orleans Lifesaving station. This was the inactive season at coastal Lifesaving stations and the Keepers and their families were usually the only ones at the stations at this time.

The Keepers of the Nauset station in Eastham and the Orleans station went to the scene of the wreck. When they arrived they found that the Keeper of the Massachusetts Humane Society house at Nauset Inlet had mustered volunteers and that they had brought the beach apparatus to the side of the wreck.

A high sea was running and waves were breaking over the stern of the ship. The crew of five and the Captain's wife found shelter in the forward section of the vessel. The volunteer Lifesaving crew managed to bring all hands ashore safely. They were taken to the Orleans station for shelter.

One week later, the schooner was tugged off the bar and towed to Boston. The *WALTER MILLER* had been bound from St. John, N.B. to New York City with a cargo of lumber under the command of Captain Barton.

The *PORTLAND*, palatial steamer between Boston, Mass. and Portland, Maine, lost on the night of November 27, 1898 with all hands and passengers. It is estimated that between one hundred fifty and two hundred people lost their lives. *Photo courtesy Peabody Museum, Salem, Mass.*

# THE PORTLAND GALE

The great gale of November 26-27, 1898 is chronologically referred to by Cape Codders as the "Portland Gale". The Lifesavers annual report called it a "Cyclonic tempest, raging with unprecedented voilence for 24 hours and with gradually abating force for 12 hours longer." Hurricane force winds at 70 MPH lashed the entire New England coastline. The seas grew higher as the storm gained in intensity. Waves reached mountainous heights and created an oceanic turbulence that tossed huge ships about like corks and - as was said in the book of Job - "The Lord maketh the deep to boil like a pot."

A storm of this magnitude causes widespread damage to even the strongest coastal ports that are fully prepared for it. A long list of vessels wrecked during this storm are entered in the Lifesaving Service records: The *COLUMBIA, CALVIN F. BAKER, MERTIS H. PERRY, ABEL E. BABCOCK, LESTER A. LEWIS, ALBERT L. BUTLER, JORDAN L. MOTT, CLARA LEAVITT* and *AMELIA G. IRELAND.* Many more were lost at sea, so the toll was heavy.

The most noted wreck during the gale was that of the steamer *PORTLAND* lost with all her crew and passengers, between 150 and 200 people. The exact number is not known as the Purser failed to report to the shipping office on India Wharf in Boston prior to sailing at 7 P.M. The *PORTLAND* was carrying a full load of Thanksgiving Holiday passengers back to Portland, Maine.

PORTLAND STEAMSHIP C©

BOSTON STEAMERS

FARE ONLY $1.00

One of the new and palatial steamers,

## "Bay State" or "Portland,"

Will leave Franklin Wharf, Portland, and India Wharf, Boston, at 7 p. m. daily, Sundays included

Through tickets can be obtained at all principal railroad stations in the State of Maine. Street cars from Union Passenger Station run to steamer dock.

J. B. COYLE,
Manager.

J. F. LISCOMB,
General Agent

**PORTLAND. MAINE.**

OPPOSITE: The Portland Plaque - Attached to the side of the Highland Lighthouse in Truro the plaque remembers the historic shipwreck off Cape Cod on Nov. 27, 1898. *Photo by Quinn* LEFT: This is a reproduction of the ship-card of the PORTLAND and her sister ship the BAY STATE. *Photo courtesy of Gordon Caldwell Hyannis.* BELOW: The wreckage of the PORTLAND washed ashore on the backside of Cape Cod from Provincetown to Chatham. Many bodies came ashore on the beaches and the wreckage was collected and set up to show the world. Shown in the photo are cabin doors, life jackets, life-boat oars, deck chairs, a boat hook, stair-railings and a quarterboard with the name Portland. *Photo courtesy of Cape Cod Photos, Orleans.*

ON NOVEMBER 27, 1898
THE STEAMER
PORTLAND
WITH 176 PERSONS ABOARD
SANK WITH NO SURVIVORS
ABOUT SEVEN MILES OUT TO
SEA FROM THIS STATION
AT CAPE COD LIGHT

THIS MEMORIAL DEDICATED NOVEMBER 27, 1948
BY THE SURVIVING MEMBERS
OF THE PORTLAND ASSOCIATES
PRESIDENT                    HISTORIAN
JOHN A. THORNQUIST        EDWARD ROWE SNOW

As the *PORTLAND* cleared Boston Harbor, scores of sailing vessels were heading in to escape the storm. Every ship in port doubled up their lines to piers, while those in the harbor dropped additional anchors. At Vineyard Haven on Martha's Vineyard, 40 ships took shelter and more than half were wrecked by the titanic power of the storm.

The *PORTLAND* sank seven miles northeast of Highland Lighthouse. Years later, her hull was found on the bottom near the hull of the schooner *ADDIE E. SNOW* which was also lost at the same time. Most of her wreckage, the ships wheel, steering cabin, quarter-boards, life preservers, and some sixty bodies of those known to be aboard, washed ashore on the outer Cape beaches between Provincetown and Chatham. Most of the wreckage came in at the northeast end of Cape Cod between Highland Lighthouse and Peaked Hill Bars. There is a plaque on the side of Highland Lighthouse, placed there by surviving relatives and friends, recalling the disaster.

The storm wrecked more ships than any other in the history of New England. There were many vessels that did not report, indicating a loss at sea. Miles of the coastline from Cape Cod to Portland, Maine were piled high with wreckage or disabled vessels, and the physical appearance of the shoreline was altered by the wind and waves. Snow was measured in feet and all communications were cut off. All telephone lines off Cape Cod were severed, and news of the *PORTLAND* wreckage ashore on the back side of Cape Cod was wired to France over the transatlantic cable in Orleans, and from there sent to New York over another cable, and thence to Boston.

The massive power of the storm can be seen in the photopraphs of the wrecks. The schooner *ALBERT L. BUTLER*, bound from Jamaica to Boston with a cargo of logwood and a crew of seven was cast ashore on Peaked Hill Bars in Provincetown and literally split in half with only one of her 3 masts standing. Three men were lost in this wreck but Lifesavers managed to save five of the crew. One of those lost was a passenger aboard the vessel.

The Schooner *ALBERT L. BUTLER* broken and aground on Peaked Hill Bars in Provincetown. The Schooner fell victim to the raging storm and three men were lost but life savers succeeded in saving five of the crew during the height of the Portland Gale. *Photo courtesy of Cape Cod Photos, Orleans.*

OPPOSITE ABOVE: Remains of *ALBERT L. BUTLER* breaking up on Peaked Hill Bars, Provincetown after Portland Gale, 1898. *Photo courtesy of a friend.* OPPOSITE BELOW: Schooners ashore in Provincetown Harbor following the Portland Gale of Nov. 27, 1898. One of these was the three masted schooner *LESTER A. LEWIS.* Wood End Life Saving Station personnel could not rescue the crew who climbed into the rigging and froze to death. *Photo courtesy of Cape Cod National Seashore.*

In Vineyard Haven harbor on Martha's Vineyard, twenty-one schooners, nearly all heavily laden, and one barkentine were driven ashore. Four schooners lying at anchor were totally dismasted. Two other schooners were sunk and one bark was resting on the bottom entirely submerged. Many other vessels driven ashore had to part their cables because of the danger of collision with other vessels which had broken adrift. Most vessels were badly battered and partially stripped of their rigging.

Vineyard Haven Harbor is normally a harbor of refuge for ships. Sometimes as many as 100 ships would seek safe anchorage to ride out a storm or just to wait until conditions were right to start the dangerous trip around Cape Cod bound for Boston, Portland or the Maritimes. The prevailing winds around Cape Cod are southwesterly and this is a fair wind for sailing vessels wishing to make passage around the Cape. A sudden wind change or a squall line spells disaster to sailing vessels too far inshore while making the passage along the backside of the Cape.

ABOVE: Vineyard Haven Harbor was badly hit during the Portland Gale. Many vessels were damaged or sunk in the harbor. The three masted British Schooner *NEWBURGH* ended up aground in front of the Seamen's Bethel. BELOW: Another British Schooner in Vineyard Haven Harbor, the *CANARIA*, aground with many other ships in the background showing the damage in the harbor. *Photos courtesy of the Vineyard Gazette, Edgartown.*

# THE MONOMOY DISASTER

The most memorable disaster involving Cape Cod Lifesavers happened on March 17, 1902 off Monomoy Island and claimed twelve lives. A northeast gale had grounded two coal barges, the *WADENA* and the *JOHN C. FITZPATRICK* on Shovelful Shoal, about one half mile off the southeastern tip of Monomoy Island south of Chatham, Mass. Wreckers were aboard the two barges for a few days and on March 17th the five men on the *WADENA* flew a distress signal to the Monomoy station. Captain Marshall W. Eldredge, keeper of the Monomoy station and seven of his crew went to the aid of the men on the *WADENA*. Mountainous seas are common to the Monomoy Point area. There are tide rips and shoals all around the tip end of Monomoy that make passage in small craft risky even in good weather.

The Lifesavers in their lifeboat arrived at the barge around noontime, took the five men off and started to row for shore. The lifeboat was difficult to handle in rough seas and shipped some water over the side. The crew of the barge panicked, stood up in the boat, grabbing the lifesavers and impeding the control of the boat. The surfboat got into the trough of the waves and tipped over, throwing all thirteen men into the raging seas. The water was ice cold and the men all had on storm clothes. The result was inevitable.

The upended boat heaved and bobbed in the tumultuous seas. Some men were lost during the initial violence of the disaster and others disappeared, one by one, until only five of the lifesavers were battling the seas trying to right their boat. Twice they had righted the craft only to have the turbulent seas capsize it again. Each coming wave claimed another victim until only one man was left, the No. 1 surfman, Seth Ellis, who hung onto the centerboard of the overturned boat but was soon exhausted himself by the ordeal.

The weather was thick with squalls and aboard the other barge Captain Elmer F. Mayo, in charge of the wrecking crew happened to glance over the side and spotted the overturned boat with four men clinging to it. The entire previous chain of events had gone unnoticed by anyone and Captain Mayo launched a dory off the *FITZPATRICK* to go to the aid of the surfmen. When he arrived, only Ellis was left atop the capsized boat. Captain Mayo saved Seth Ellis in those high seas, brought him ashore and both men lived to tell the tale of the Monomoy Disaster.

Excerpts from the U. S. Life Saving Service report for the fiscal year ending June 30, 1902 state:

"By far the most distressing calamity to the Life Saving Service during many years, and one unequaled by more than two or three in its history, was that which occurred on the 17th of March, 1902, near the eastern end of Shovelful Shoal, coast of Massachusetts, and resulted in the drowning of 12 persons, 5 from the stranded coal barge *WADENA* and 7 from the crew of the Monomoy Lifesaving station.*

"When Captain Mayo left the *FITZPATRICK* on this self-imposed perilous mission of humanity he was warned that he would never live to accomplish it, and when it was done, and tidings of it spread abroad, it was proclaimed throughout the land as from beginning to end a most noble and brilliant achievement. In recognition of his extraordinary merits the Secretary of the Treasury, therefore, bestowed upon him the gold life-saving medal, which may be awarded only to those who display the most extreme and heroic daring in saving life from the perils of the sea. Surfman Ellis, for his devotion to duty, his faultless courage, and self-sacrificing fidelity to his comrades, was likewise honored, and promoted to the keepership of his station.

---

* The Monomoy Lifesaving station was situated at what is now the midway point (see map pg. 64) down the six mile long sand spit. The Monomoy Point station was built later in 1903.

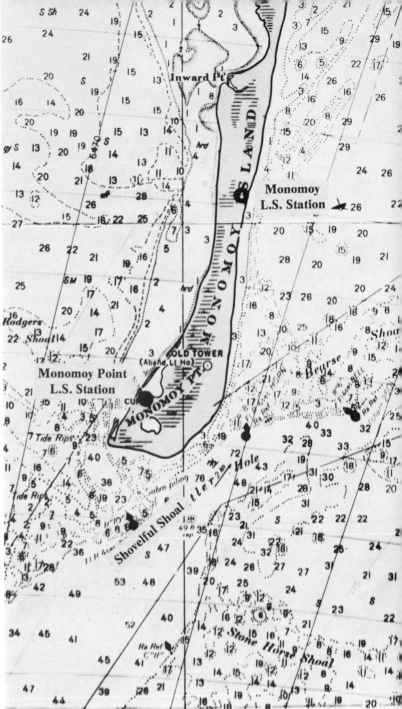

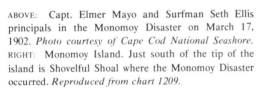

ABOVE: Capt. Elmer Mayo and Surfman Seth Ellis principals in the Monomoy Disaster on March 17, 1902. *Photo courtesy of Cape Cod National Seashore.*
RIGHT: Monomoy Island. Just south of the tip of the island is Shovelful Shoal where the Monomoy Disaster occurred. *Reproduced from chart 1209.*

"The loss of the 7 Lifesaving men who so nobly perished created everywhere a sense of profound sorrow. There was no more skillful or fearless crew on the whole coast, and since it appeared that the WADENA remained safe for days after the disaster, there was a general conviction that the men were practically a sacrifice, on the one hand to the needless apprehensions and senseless panic of the men from the barge, and on the other to their own high sense of duty, which would not permit them to turn their backs upon a signal of distress. "We must go" said the keeper; "there is a distress flag in the rigging."

Throughout the country, feelings of sorrow and sympathy were expressed for the surviving widows and orphans of the twelve men. In Massachusetts a fund drive to aid the families of the men raised over $45,000. Memorial services were held throughout the Cape at the time. Today a tall monument stands in Chatham, next to the Coast Guard station, as a memorial to the men who were lost in the disaster that fateful day off Monomoy in 1902.

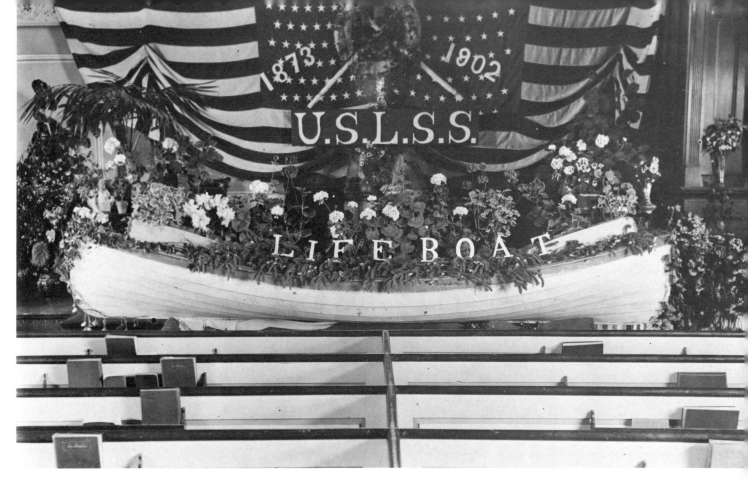

ABOVE: Memorial Services were held at the Orleans Congregational Church for those who lost their lives in the Monomoy Disaster on March 17, 1902. *Photo by H. K. Cummings, Orleans.*

ABOVE: This monument in Chatham beside the Coast Guard Station is dedicated to memory of those who perished in the Monomoy Disaster, March 17, 1902. BELOW: Close up view of the back face of the monument outlining the rescue and the event. *Photos by Quinn*

IN MEMORY OF
THE HERO OF THE MONOMOY DISASTER
1862 CAPTAIN ELMER F. MAYO 1935
CHATHAM, MASS.
AND HIS GALLANT RESCUE OF
SURFMAN SETH L. ELLIS
FROM A WATERY GRAVE ON SHOVELFUL SHOAL
OFF MONOMOY POINT
MARCH 17, 1902

IN MEMORY OF
1858 SURFMAN SETH L. ELLIS 1935
HARWICHPORT, MASS.
SOLE SURVIVOR OF THE U. S. LIFE SAVING CREW
IN THEIR HEROIC ATTEMPT TO
RESCUE THE IMPERILED CREW
OF THE BARGE WADENA

Aerial view of Monomoy Island taken from high over Chatham looking south with Nantucket Island in the distance. The rip tides and currents still broil off the tip of Monomoy to this day.
*Aerial photograph by Richard Cooper Kelsey, Chatham, Mass.*

ABOVE: The *CITY OF COLUMBUS* sunk off Devil's Bridge just off the Gay Head Cliffs. Martha's Vineyard with a loss of 103 lives. *Photo courtesy of the Vineyard Gazette, Edgartown, Mass.* BELOW: On July 18, 1886 the Steamer *GATE CITY* ran aground on Naushon Island, southwest of Cape Cod in dense fog. The Boston-Savannah vessel was loaded with watermelons. The unfortunate vessel with a history of many mishaps ran aground just a few miles from Devil's Bridge where her sister ship the *CITY OF COLUMBUS* was wrecked on January 17, 1884. Her bow, with a rock piercing the hull, rested 150 feet off shore with her stern in 25 feet of water. Thousands of watermelons were dumped overboard to lighten the vessel. She was refloated a week later. *Photo courtesy of the Mariners Museum, Newport News, Virginia.*

# CHAPTER 4

**The Iron Ships.
As the steamer replaced the sailing ship, the iron
ships began to appear on the beaches of Cape Cod.**

Down toward the end of the 19th century the white sails began to thin out on the horizons off Cape Cod. The handwriting was on the bulkhead and a new era in seafaring was coming into being. Steamships had power that did not depend on the capricious winds.

The sailing vessel continued however in the coastal trades but many large barks and schooners became barges, tethered by towlines to steam tugs. The coastal trade continued until the depression in the 1930's when the lack of business mired the wooden hulls in muddy anchorages all along the coast.

Man's fallibility was as consistent with his new iron ships as it had been with the wooden sailing vessels. Many steamships met with accidents while passing around the Cape. On January 17, 1884 the steamer *CITY OF COLUMBUS*, 1,992 tons, steamed out of Boston bound for Savanah, Georgia with 87 passengers headed for the winter in Florida. Early in the morning of the 18th the steamer made an error in dead reckoning and came to grief on Devil's Bridge at Gay Head on Martha's Vineyard Island.

The ship ran up on the rocks and stove a hole in her bottom. She did not hit hard, and her Captain believed that damage was minimal so he decided to back off the rocks. The vessel had suffered a fatal blow when she fetched up on the ledge. When she backed off, water came pouring into the hold and she settled quickly carrying many people to their deaths.

Of the 87 passengers and 45 crewmen, 103 people died. Many died from exposure, as Livesavers from Martha's Vineyard tried to save people frozen in the rigging. Many more leaped to their deaths in the frigid waters of Vineyard Sound. More were drowned in their cabins still in their night clothes. A court of inquiry found Captain S. E. Wright negligent and revoked his license.

The Yacht *ALVA* was built in 1886 for millionaire William K. Vanderbilt and was 285 feet long, rigged as a three masted topsail schooner but with steam power and a cruising speed of 15 knots, built at a cost of $500,000. The *ALVA* was named after Vanderbilt's wife and was on her way from Bar Harbor, Maine to Newport, R. I. when early in the morning of July 23, 1892 she became fog bound in Pollock Rip Slue, east of Chatham. The Captain of the *ALVA* decided not to run through the channel in the dense fog and instead anchored at about 6 A.M., to wait out the weather. At 8 A.M. the Boston-New York steamer *H. F. DIMOCK* loomed out of the fog and headed directly for the *ALVA*.

There was less than 100 yards between the two vessels and there was no time to alter course on the *DIMOCK*. The *ALVA* was struck on the port side near the stern. The collision ripped steel plates right down below the water line. Mr. Vanderbilt and his guests were all asleep at the time of the accident and were rudely awakened by stewards who rushed them on

69

ABOVE: The Boston-New York steamer *H. F. DIMOCK* which sank the Yacht *ALVA* that foggy morning out in the Pollock Rip Channel. In addition to the *ALVA*, the *DIMOCK* also sank the Steamer *HORATIO HALL*, March 10, 1909 near the same spot. The *DIMOCK* suffered damage then and had to be beached on Nauset Beach for temporary repairs, however she went back to sea and became one of the first large ships to pass through the Cape Cod Canal after it opened in 1915. OPPOSITE ABOVE: The Vanderbilt Yacht *ALVA*, biggest and most costly yacht afloat in 1892. She was rammed and sunk by the Boston-New York steamer *H. F. DIMOCK* in Pollock Rip Channel on a hot July day in 1892. OPPOSITE BELOW: Pollock Rip Channel, August 8, 1892 showing the *ALVA* on the bottom with just the tops of the masts showing. Note the horizon full of sails of pleasure yachts. In good weather, a trip out to the wreck was a full day's outing for family and friends. *Photos courtesy of Peabody Museum, Salem, Mass.*

deck in their pajamas and robes to be loaded into the ship's boats which had been lowered just after the collision. The *ALVA* filled quickly and started to settle minutes after the accident. The entire ship's company was taken aboard the *H. F. DIMOCK* which suffered extensive damage to her bow plates but still able to remain afloat. The *DIMOCK* was at the scene until just after noon and then continued on her trip to Boston where Mr. Vanderbilt, after landing was immediately on the telegraph to arrange for a new yacht.

The *ALVA* stayed on the bottom of Pollock Rip Slue and four days later on July 27th the schooner *EVERETT WEBSTER* sailing from Philadelphia, Pa., to Salem, Mass., with a cargo of 707 tons of coal ran up on her sunken hull. The collision carried away the *ALVA*'s fore topmast and smokestack and left the schooner hung up on the yacht. The tug *JOSHUA LOVETT* pulled the *WEBSTER* off the *ALVA* and then proceeded to tow her into Salem with four feet of water in her hold. The *WEBSTER* was a small two masted schooner, 140 feet long with a 35 foot beam.

Soon after, the hull of the *ALVA* was considered a menace to navigation and had to be blown up to clear the shipping lanes. The *DIMOCK* went back to her Boston-New York run and enjoyed a quiet existance for 17 years. In 1909, the *DIMOCK* rammed another steamer, the *HORATIO HALL*, again in pea soup fog, and again in Pollock Rip Slue. The *HALL* was sunk and the *DIMOCK* suffered such damage to her bow plates that she had to beach herself until repairs could be made to her bow to prevent her sinking.

The wooden steamer *LONGFELLOW* steaming out of Provincetown Harbor for Boston. *Photo courtesy of Cape Cod Photos, Orleans.*

The wooden steamer *LONGFELLOW* (named after the poet) was 413 tons and carried on packet service between Provincetown and Boston from 1883 until 1903. After finishing her career as an excursion vessel she went into the freight service and was carrying a load of explosives to the Portsmouth Navy Yard in New Hampshire from Wilmington, Delaware when off Cape Cod she started leaking. The crew fought for 24 hours to keep the Longfellow afloat but had to abandon her four miles off Highland Lighthouse on September 9, 1904. The crew left the sinking steamer in the two lifeboats and with much difficulty managed to land on Cape Cod with the aid of the U. S. Lifesaving service boats which came out to assist them.

There were some feeble attempts at salvage but the potential nature of the cargo discouraged many from going anywhere near the sunken hull. Two months later, on November 13, a severe gale started blowing and the sunken hull began pounding on the bottom. Two gigantic explosions shook the lower Cape, the first at 7:45 P.M. and the second 8 P.M. The beach was littered with dead fish, killed by the two blasts. Later pieces of the wooden framing, planking, masts and other wreckage littered the shoreline from Peaked Hill Bars to Eastham. The modern steamer *CAPE COD* replaced the *LONGFELLOW* on the Provincetown-Boston run and stayed in service for many years.

On January 13, 1907 the American Steamer *ONONDAGA* stranded on Nauset Beach in Chatham in dense fog. In order to remove the steamer from the beach she had to be unloaded by local help. *Photo loaned by Howard W. Quinn.*

On January 13, 1907 the American steamer *ONONDAGA*, 2,696 tons, Boston to Jacksonville, Florida with Captain Bunnell commanding, stranded at 1:30 A.M., 1½ miles north of the Old Harbor station in thick fog. A high sea was running and warning was given by the lookout. The Lifesavers went to the aid of the stranded liner. The first shot from the Lyle gun landed a line on her deck and the Lifesavers hauled out the breeches buoy, but the steamer was in no danger and none of her crew were landed.

The weather moderated and the Lifesavers were reduced to the role of errand boys carrying messages, back and forth, and ferrying underwriter's agents to the grounded ship. The *ONONDAGA* lay on the sand for three months until on March 14, 1907, with the assistance of tugboats, the steamer was refloated.

The *ONONDAGA* came ashore with a cargo valued at $160,000. The cargo had to be removed in order to refloat the vessel. This necessitated hiring local help to transfer the cargo to the rail freight station in Orleans. During the transfer of wrapping paper, shoes, screen doors and other mixed cargo, a loss of $68,905 in goods was reported. Needless to say, the children of the lower Cape were well fitted with new shoes that year. Anonymous reports confirm that there is still some wrapping paper hidden away in some lower Cape attics to this day from the wreck of the *ONONDAGA*. On June 28, 1918, the *ONONDAGA* sank on the rocks off Sugar Reef, Watch Hill, Rhode Island while she was headed for France with a general cargo.

73

ABOVE: Workmen unload the big steamer by hand. It took days to complete the job that would take only hours today with modern machinery, but it enabled the local workers to appropriate out of a $160,000 cargo $68,905 worth of extra pay for their efforts. *Photo loaned by Howard W. Quinn.* BELOW: *ONONDAGA*, turned around, with two men digging clams inshore of wreck with lighter and tug off shore. Photo was probably just before the ship was removed from the beach. *Photo courtesy of Tales of Cape Cod, Inc. Barnstable.*

ABOVE: The *HORATIO HALL* which was struck and sunk by the Steamer *H. F. DIMOCK* on March 10, 1909 in Pollock Rip Channel off Chatham, Mass. *Photo courtesy of Peabody Museum, Salem.* BELOW: The *HORATIO HALL* after being rammed by the *H. F. DIMOCK* in fog. Note hole in hull by the stern mast. The *HALL* was built 1898 at Chester, Pa. by the Delaware River Co. and owned by the Maine S.S. Co. 3,168 tons, 297' long. *Photo courtesy of Mariners Museum, Newport News, Va.*

The dense Cape Cod fog caused another steamer disaster on March 10, 1909 when the Boston-New York steamer *H. F. DIMOCK* collided with the steamer *HORATIO HALL* in Pollock Rip Slue off Chatham. The *DIMOCK* could not be seen from shore because of the fog, but her distress signals were heard at the Orleans Life Saving station.

Lifesavers launched a lifeboat and rowed to the side of the *DIMOCK*. Following the collision, the passengers and crew of the *HORATIO HALL* had gone aboard the *DIMOCK* and the *HALL* sank on Pollock Rip Shoals with her superstructure still above water. The *DIMOCK* had sustained hull damage in her bow section and was in danger of sinking so the Lifesavers landed a boatload of survivors and requested help from the Nauset and Chatham stations in saving the remainder of the people aboard the foundering steamer.

ABOVE: The *H. F. DIMOCK* ashore at Orleans, note the patch on her bow. This photo was made just prior to refloating on March 14, 1909. *Photo courtesy of Tales of Cape Cod, Inc., Barnstable.*

OPPOSITE: The Italian Bark *CASTAGNA* ashore at Wellfleet on Feb. 17, 1914. Iron hulled bark was wrecked in a storm and five of the thirteen crewmen perished of the cold. *Photo by Boston Post, courtesy Albert E. Snow, Orleans.*

The work of rescue was continued and 67 persons were landed. The seas had driven the steamer so close to shore that it was now within reach of the beach apparatus, so the Captain and crew remained on board. The decision was made to beach the *DIMOCK* to prevent her loss. She was run ashore ½ mile south of the Orleans station.

The *H. F. DIMOCK* was refloated on March 14th after repairs had been made to the bow section to insure against sinking and she was towed to Boston. The *HORATIO HALL* was declared a menace to navigation and had to be blown up. Her quarterboard and many other articles are still in Chatham. The *HALL* was the second vessel the *DIMOCK* had sunk on Pollock Rip Shoals. There were some moves toward declaring the *DIMOCK* a menace to navigation around the Chatham roads area of the Atlantic Ocean.

Many of the iron ships still employed sails, and the wind was still free for economy minded owners where time was not a factor in delivery of a cargo. A major disaster to an iron hulled sail vessel occurred on February 17, 1914 in Wellfleet when the 843 ton Italian Bark *CASTAGNA* went ashore early in the morning while enroute from Montevideo, Uruguay to Weymouth, Massachusetts with a cargo of guano.

76

The freezing temperatures caused the men aboard the bark extreme suffering before Lifesavers could effect their rescue. Four men froze to death in the rigging before they could be saved. Lifesavers from the Cahoon's Hollow and Nauset stations assisted the crew of the bark.

One of the factors in the loss of life was that the sailors all wore summer clothing and had not been provided with even storm garments. The Lifesavers removed the eight survivors and rushed them up the beach to the nearest shelter, which at that time was the Marconi Radio Station on a high bluff overlooking the ocean in Wellfleet. There, in the warmth of the station, the sufferers were rubbed down and brought back to life and later that afternoon were taken to a hospital in Boston.

The wireless towers at the Marconi Radio Station Wellfleet where the frost-bitten crewmen of the *CASTAGNA* were taken for shelter following the wreck. *Photo courtesy of John Bell, Provincetown.*

The *CASTAGNA* hull is still sanded in, a short way off the beach, underwater. The Marconi Radio station was in service for only a short period of time and then closed down. However, they successfully transmitted the first trans-Atlantic radio message while in operation. The few remains of the station have been preserved by the Cape Cod National Seashore with suitable plaques and information about the early pioneers in the radio field.

In the following year, there was a major change in the Life Saving service. The Revenue Cutter Service and the Life Saving Service were combined into one unit on January 28, 1915 and became the United States Coast Guard. The combining of the two services was a natural move as better co-ordination between shore and sea units resulted in a high degree of efficiency in operations of the life saving field.

The arrival of the steam age made the sailing ship almost obsolete. Many of the hulls could carry large cargoes and by stringing two or three behind a steam tug, an economical combination resulted. As long as the weather was good the system worked well but when stormy conditions came up, the marriage of steam and sail craft sometimes ended up on the rocks.

On April 4, 1915, three barges were in tow of the tug *MARS* from Bangor, Maine to Philadelphia, Pa., and they ran into a fierce storm off Cape Cod. The tug was unable to fight the storm and had to cast off the three barges to save herself. The barges ended up on the beach in Truro right in front of the Highland Coast Guard station.

The *COLERAINE*, the *TUNNEL RIDGE*, and the *MANHEIM* were lined up along the front of the beach in a helter skelter pattern. The *COLERAINE* and the *TUNNEL RIDGE* were broadside of the surf and suffered damage to their hulls, they were declared total losses. The *MANHEIM* came in stern first with her bow to the sea, and was not damaged at all. The *MANHEIM* however, was to lay on the beach in Truro for one year before she could be removed.

The job of salvage on the other two barges was underway immediately and the little house on top of the barge *COLERAINE* was removed and brought to the top of the cliff near Highland Lighthouse and became a golf pro shop for the Highland Golf Course. The hulls of the two barges were burned after all cargo of value had been removed from them. On April 4, 1916 the Barge *MANHEIM* was floated off the sandy shores of Cape Cod and went back into the coal transportation business.

ABOVE: Left to Right, the barges *MANHEIM, TUNNEL RIDGE* and *COLERAINE* ashore at the Highland Station in Truro. The vessels grounded during a storm on April 4, 1915. *Photo by Small, Buzzards Bay, Mass.* BELOW: The pilot house of the barge *COLERAINE* which was removed from the wreck and brought up from the beach to the Highland House to serve as a clubhouse for the golf links in Truro overlooking the Atlantic Ocean.

ABOVE: Brigantine *POINSETT* ashore near Nobadeer Pond, on Nantucket Island on August 30, 1870. Some of her cargo of sugar was salvaged but the ship became a total wreck. *From the collection of Paul C. Morris, Nantucket, Mass.* BELOW: Late in the evening of August 22, 1884, the *U.S.S. TALLAPOOSA*, a sidewheel Navy steamer, was rammed and sunk in Vineyard Sound by the coal laden schooner *JAMES S. LOWELL* of Bath, Maine. The accident occurred on a clear night, and witnesses claimed that both vessels saw the lights of the other. The *LOWELL* and other vessels picked up the crew of the steamer, which went down in ten minutes. Three of the crew of the Naval vessel were lost. The ship was raised and repaired in the New York Naval Shipyard. *Photo by Baldwin Coolidge, courtesy of the Society for the Preservation of New England Antiquities, Boston, Massachusetts.*

# CHAPTER 5

**Wrecks around the Islands.
Down through the years, the storms and fogs of Nantucket and
Martha's Vineyard have taken a heavy toll of ships.**

The Bark *W. F. MARSHALL*, ashore on the south side of Nantucket Island on March 9, 1877. *From the collection of Paul C. Morris, Nantucket.*

They call her "The Little Gray Lady of the Sea". Ben Franklin's mother was born here in 1667 and in the 18th century, Nantucket was the whaling center of the world with 150 ships and 2,000 sailors. The annual product exceeded 30,000 barrels of sperm oil. A few miles off the south coast of Cape Cod are the islands of Nantucket and Martha's Vineyard. Around these islands are a checkerboard of shoals. Currents surge around the reefs brewing disaster for ships trying to reach open waters.

The shoal areas are dangerous, their names loom ominously up out of the depths, Devil's Bridge, Cross Rip shoal, Hedge Fence shoal, Old Man shoal and Miacomet Rip. These are but a few of the sites of shipwrecks that have occurred around these islands. In early times Nantucket exported huge amounts of whale oil and imported all trade goods. The shipping lanes were well known but the ship groundings were as numerous here as on Cape Cod, one of which was the two masted schooner *OREGON*, 92 tons, bound from Bay View, Massachusetts to New Bedford with a cargo of granite blocks. The *OREGON* was battling heavy swells off Nantucket on August 25, 1885 with rough seas and a strong northwest wind. The crew ran the ship onto the beach at Squam Head to prevent her from sinking in off-shore waters. The Keeper of the Coskata station arrived at the scene but the schooner was beyond help. The cargo was salvaged but the ship was a total loss.

ABOVE: Schooner *AUSTEN LOCKE* ashore on the south side of Nantucket Island near Miacomet Pond on Dec. 9, 1885, her cargo of salt was saved before she broke up. OPPOSITE: The Schooner *OREGON* ashore at Wauwinet, Nantucket Island on Aug. 25, 1885 with a cargo of granite. The cargo was salvaged and the ship broke up. *Photos from the collection of Paul C. Morris, Nantucket.*

It was foggy and raining at an hour before midnight on December 9, 1885 when the western patrol from the Surfside station spotted a wreck on the outer bar at an area west of Miacomet Pond. There was a strong southerly wind at the time and the Lifesaver burned his coston signal to alert the crew of the vessel that help was on the way. When the crew of the Surfside station arrived with the beach cart the surf had worked the schooner over the outer bar and nearer shore. The mountainous waves discouraged the ship's crew from launching a boat and Lifesavers landed a shot line on board and removed the crew of six by breeches buoy.

The information related to the Lifesavers when the crew reached shore was that the ship was the Nova Scotia schooner *AUSTEN LOCKE*, bound from Anguilla, B.W.I. to Portland, Maine with a cargo of salt. The Captain said that he had become lost in the fog. The next day, Lifesavers went aboard the vessel and saved the crew's clothing and the ship's instruments but the ship was a total loss. Part of the cargo was salvaged.

83

The Ship *ANTOINETTE*, Montevideo to Boston in ballast went ashore on Tuckernuck Island west of Nantucket on January 27, 1889 and her crew was rescued by the Life Savers by breeches buoy. *From the collection of Paul C. Morris, Nantucket.*

The elements gave the Lifesavers a merry chase during the wreck of the British ship *ANTOINETTE* on the foggy night of January 27, 1889. The ship was out of her bearings and lost in dense fog when she came ashore on Tuckernuck Island, west of Nantucket.

The night patrol from the Muskeget station on an adjacent island spotted torches through the fog that the crew of the vessel had ignited as a distress signal.

When the ship struck, a high surf was battering the hull and Captain Ferguson decided to cut the mainmast away. While this was being carried out the other two masts were pulled down with the connecting lines.

The crew of the Muskeget station were unable to bring their surfboat to the scene because of the low tide between the islands, so they came over in dories and arrived at the wreck at midnight.

A rough sea was running and the Lifesavers decided that a surfboat was needed to effect the rescue of the people aboard the ship. They went to the Massachusetts Humane Society boathouse which was about a mile from the scene and discovered that an ox team would be needed to pull the boat back to the wreck. There were no tractors in those days. After much delay, they procured the services of a team of oxen and the boat was pulled back to the wreck. During the delay, the wind and tide had risen making the surf impassable. With the high tide however, they were able to go back to the Muskeget station on the other island and obtain the beach apparatus and return to Tuckernuck Island to try to rescue the crew of the stranded vessel.

They arrived back at sunrise and immediately began the work of removing the people from the wreck. After one crewman had been landed, the whip line of the apparatus fouled and had to be cleared before any further operations could proceed. Surfman Coffin went out to the ship and cleared the lines and then the entire company of 20 people, including 2 women, were landed.

Captain Ferguson related that he couldn't get any bearings for several days and believed that his ship was east of the South-shoal lightship. The elements seemed to be against the rescue of the souls aboard the *ANTOINETTE* but the persevering and duty-bound Lifesavers would not be swayed by Mother Nature's conspiracy and they pressed on, never allowing their many setbacks from achieving their ultimate goal. The *ANTOINETTE* was in ballast so no cargo was salvaged and the vessel became a total wreck.

The Barkentine *CULDOON* bound from Capetown to Boston ran ashore in thick fog at Nobadeer on Nantucket Island on March 23, 1898. BELOW: The Barkentine *CULDOON* ashore at Nobadeer Nantucket shortly before being hauled off March 26th, 1898. *Photos from the collection of Paul C. Morris.*

The notorious Nantucket fog stranded the Barkentine *CULDOON* at Nobadeer on March 23, 1898. The *CULDOON* bound from Capetown to Boston with a cargo of wool had her foremast snapped in half when she struck the shore. She went aground early in the morning a mile east of the Surfside Lifesaving station and when the Lifesavers arrived, the crew of nine landed in the ship's boat. The mate had been injured when the boat landed in the surf, and was taken to the station for treatment. The cargo was unloaded and on March 26, the tug *RIGHT ARM* pulled the 424 ton *CULDOON* off and towed her to Boston.

# THE JENNIE FRENCH POTTER

At the turn of the century, five masted schooners began to appear on the east coast. They were bigger and could carry more cargo. A bigger ship obviously led to a bigger shipwreck. The *JENNIE FRENCH POTTER* was a five masted schooner loaded with coal bound from Newport News, Virginia to Boston and passed the Vineyard on May 16, 1909 heading easterly. Due to the light winds she anchored near the *CROSS RIP LIGHTSHIP* to wait favorable conditions.

The vessel got underway at dawn on Tuesday the 18th and Captain Charles Potter, who was one of the owners, set a course for the *HANDKERCHIEF LIGHTSHIP*. The wind was still light and the tide was running stronger than the wind and carried the ship to the northern side of the channel where she struck the tail of Half Moon Shoal and grounded.

Sometime later, the crew found that the vessel was taking on water and filling rapidly. At this time the tug *FRED E. RICHARDS* approached the *JENNIE FRENCH POTTER* from the westward and Captain Potter and his two daughters went aboard the tug and were brought into Vineyard Haven. The crew remained aboard the schooner.

Captain Potter immediately telegraphed for a wrecking firm and efforts to refloat the ship began on Wednesday, May 19th. The tug *ORION* arrived in Vineyard Haven and picked up the Captain and two divers and went to Half Moon Shoal where she joined the tugs *UNDERWRITER* and *CONFIDENCE*, along with the wrecking lighter *SALVOR* from Boston.

The *JENNIE FRENCH POTTER* was built in Camden, Maine in 1899 and hailed from New york. She was 1,794 tons and was, fortunately, insured, as the hull still lies, sanded in on Half Moon Shoal in the center of Nantucket Sound.

OPPOSITE: The five masted schooner *JENNIE FRENCH POTTER*, sunk in Nantucket Sound on May 18, 1909. BELOW: The *JENNIE FRENCH POTTER*, broadside quarter view. *Photos from the collection of Paul C. Morris, Nantucket.*

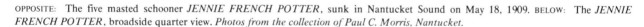

The fishing schooner *MAUD SEWARD* ashore at North Tisbury on Martha's Vineyard, Jan. 30, 1910. *Photo courtesy of Vineyard Gazette, Edgartown.*

The two masted schooner *BASILE* of Weymouth, N. S. came ashore on March 22, 1913 on the South Beach of Martha's Vineyard ten miles ESE of the Gay Head life saving station. The *BASILE* was a total loss. *Photo courtesy of Vineyard Gazette, Edgartown.*

The Hedge Fence, Squash Meadow and Middle Ground Shoals were, to sailors headed for Vineyard Haven harbor, what a few well placed sand traps around a green are to a golfer today. Martha's Vineyard is the larger of the two islands. Vineyard Haven was once known as Holmes Holl and sometimes the schooner masts made the harbor look like a forest.

On January 30, 1910 with a gale screaming through her rigging, the schooner *MAUD SEWARD,* bound from New York City to Provincetown with a cargo of 290 tons of coal, parted her mooring off Chatham and was blown over the shoals into the sound. The schooner, adrift all night, was carried into Vineyard Sound. She came aground just west of Cedar Tree Neck. Captain Joseph Norton ordered his crew of four into the ship's dory and they made it ashore where they walked to the Obed Daggett house for shelter. The crew were taken to the Seamen's Bethel in Vineyard Haven on the following day.

On March 22, 1913 the two masted British schooner *BASILE* of Weymouth, Nova Scotia was underway in fog and drove herself up on the South Beach of Martha's Vineyard. The schooner, bound from Haiti to Nova Scotia without any cargo, was riding high in the water and she grounded so high on the sands that the crew was able to leap ashore and not get their feet wet. The vessel was not damaged but salvage was impossible. The wreck was too far inshore to bring tugs for the tow off the sand. She went to pieces on the beach and was a total wreck.

ABOVE: The Fishing schooner *EVELYN M. THOMPSON*, wrecked at Low Beach, Nantucket Island on July 14, 1918. BELOW: The wreckage of the *HENRY F. KREGER*, a four masted schooner that struck on Little Round Shoal, east of Nantucket on Oct. 26, 1921 and was a total loss. The crew was rescued by the Coskata Coast Guard. The after section of the vessel broke loose and drifted in near Cisco, South Shore on Nantucket. *Photos from the collection of Paul C. Morris, Nantucket.*

The *CROSS RIP LIGHTSHIP.* Heavy ice fields wrenched the ship from its moorings on February 1, 1918 and carried it out to sea. Neither the ship, nor her crew of six, has ever been seen since. *From the collection of Paul C. Morris, Nantucket, Mass.*

Ice conditions in the winter of 1918 in Nantucket Sound were at their worst. On February 1, 1918, ice built up and the tide wrenched the *CROSS RIP LIGHTSHIP* from her moorings and held her tight in the ice field. The ship was without sail or power. She had no radio communications on board and could do nothing to help herself out of the frozen field.

The tide carried the vessel back and forth in the sound for a few days but rescue was impossible. She could not be reached by cutters or tugs and on February 5th, the ice field moved out to sea and the Lightship was last seen from the Great Point Lighthouse flying a distress signal; her crew of six on deck. She disappeared over the horizon and was never seen again.

ABOVE: On April 26, 1924 the New Bedford Whaling Bark *WANDERER* was driven ashore at Cuttyhunk during one of the worst storms in the history of the island. The crew was saved. *Photo courtesy of Peabody Museum, Salem.*

BELOW: Cuttyhunk Island is the last of the Elizabeth chain which stretches from Woods Hole down to the end of Buzzards Bay.

On April 26, 1924, part of the New Bedford whaling industry ended on the shore of Cuttyhunk Island in the Elizabeth Island chain. During one of the worst storms in the history of Cuttyhunk the New Bedford Bark *WANDERER* was driven ashore and wrecked.

The *WANDERER* was the last square rigged whaling vessel to sail from the port of New Bedford. Soon after she hit, two boats put off from the vessel with the crew. One boat contained eight men and the other had six.

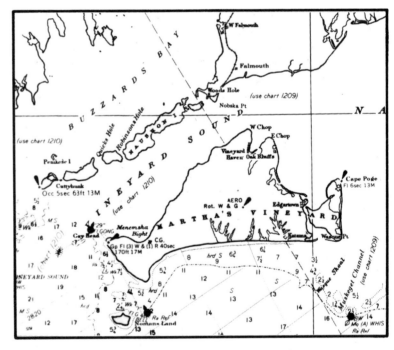

From a cliff on the shore, observers could see that the latter boat appeared to be making a losing fight.

Five men from Cuttyhunk put out from the lee of the island and endeavored to reach the men from the bark. Before they could get to the boats however, the boat with six men had been assisted through the high surf and the other boat had disappeared. The Cuttyhunkers learned afterwards that the boat had reached the *VINEYARD SOUND LIGHTSHIP.*

The ship was a total wreck and was soon stripped by wreckers. The *WANDERER* was built in Mattapoisett in 1878.

# CHAPTER 6

**The history, construction and opening of the Cape Cod Canal at the beginning of the 20th century. Some early wrecks in the canal and some modern canal views.**

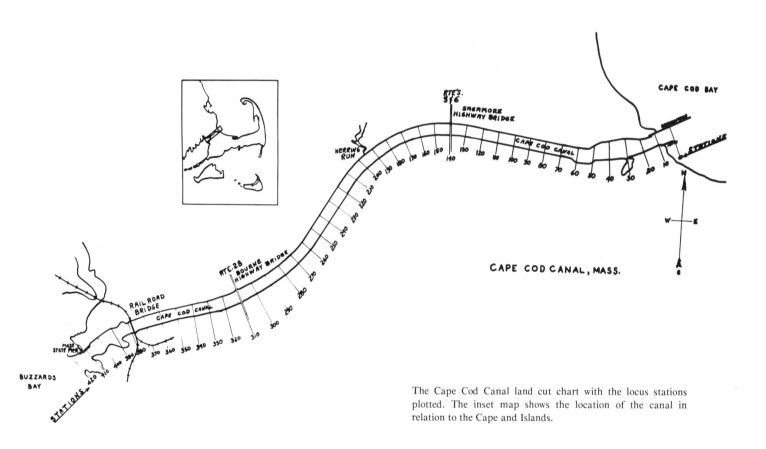

The Cape Cod Canal land cut chart with the locus stations plotted. The inset map shows the location of the canal in relation to the Cape and Islands.

The shipwrecks, the Lifesavers, the Mooncussers, the Wreckers, the fog and the storms have all contributed to the early photographs in this book. In the early 1600's a water passage from Cape Cod Bay to Buzzards Bay had been proposed by Miles Standish of the Plymouth Colony. Down through the years, many proposals urged the digging of the "Ship Canal" in the upper Cape area.

Perhaps the politics of the day prevailed, just as they do today, where greed and profit are the paramount concern to the individuals involved in the project. However, August Belmont, a noted financier, became interested in the canal project and with his backing the job got underway. With the engineering abilities of William Parsons, five years after the digging started, they opened the canal to limited ship traffic.

93

Portrait of August Belmont. Belmont was the man who obtained the capital to build the canal and saw the project through to completion after others had failed. *Photo courtesy of Ben Harrison, Buzzards Bay.*

Chief Engineer William Parsons. With the financing of Belmont and the engineering know-how of Parsons, a canal was completed joining the waters of Cape Cod Bay and Buzzards Bay, changing the mileage for shipping between New York & Boston and saving seventy miles sailing. *Photo courtesy of Ben Harrison, Buzzards Bay.*

The long sought answer to the problems of shipwrecks on the backside of Cape Cod had been found. In theory this was partially correct. However, large ships and sailing vessels without auxiliary power were unable to pass through the canal which was only 18 feet deep, and 100 feet wide. The wrecks continued on the outer Cape beaches. Their number dwindled somewhat but nevertheless the wrecks still occurred.

Mr. Benjamin S. Harrison, a well known photographer and lecturer from Buzzards Bay, recently retired from the Cape Cod Canal operations as a traffic dispatcher and he has prepared a chronological history of the waterway beginning with the proposal of Miles Standish and coming down to the present day. This history is concise, factual and complete.

Along with Mr. Harrison's collection of photographs of the construction and opening of the canal, the history is presented here:

The Cape Cod Canal, located 50 miles south of Boston, Massachusetts, one of the most important waterways in the world, has a history dating back to 1623. This date seems unimportant when we consider that canals and rivers were the earliest means of transportation known to man. Prior to that the range of travel had been limited to forest trails and tribal communications confined to immediate neighborhoods. So far as we know, Captain Miles Standish of the Plymouth Bay Colony, in 1623 was the first man to envision a canal connecting the waters of Cape Cod Bay and Buzzards Bay. His idea being to expedite and facilitate commerce between the Dutch of New Amsterdam and the Pilgrims of Plymouth Colony.

He at that time chose the route for the Canal that eventually was used in the actual construction. Three other routes for canals across Cape Cod were proposed in later years. In 1627 Governor Bradford and Miles Standish followed through with this same proposal, same route, and at that time the Dutch Trading Post, Aptuxet, was built. The name Aptuxet in the Indian tongue means "trail of the burden carriers." This trading post has been perpetuated for the people of today to visit and is one of the attractions for tourists on Cape Cod.

ABOVE: Construction is begun with the land cut. This photo was taken at station 270 looking east on the Cape side. Tracks are laid on the floor of the cut and trains carry out the material dug by power shovels and laborers. BELOW: The cut gets deeper into the cape as this photograph shows, looking west from station 250 on the Cape side. *Photos courtesy of Ben Harrison, Buzzards Bay.*

ABOVE: The digging became a huge operation as the work continued. This was at station 280 looking east on the mainland side. Bournedale is in the upper left center of the photo. BELOW: Large steam shovels at work removing material from the bottom of the canal. *Photos by Fred Small, courtesy of Bourne Historical Society.*

The job of removing the earth was carried out using railroad cars and small work engines at station 280 looking east on the mainland side. *Photo by Fred Small, courtesy of Bourne Historical Society.*

On September 2, 1627, after an extremely bad winter, when the Plymouth Colony was threatened with starvation, Miles Standish sailed his shallops towards the country of the Shawmes. Thence, with his boats pulling up the Scusset River, as far as possible, he took his crew to a high point of only 29 feet above the sea and in the distance saw before him in Monument or Manomet River, a small flotilla. This group of vessels was under Issac De Resieres from New Amsterdam. The Dutch had come to this point, as far to the east as they could get in this river, to relieve the starving pilgrims.

The first commerce between the Dutch and Plymouth Bay Colony began on the line of the present day Canal. Several proposals and surveys were made from this time over the years until the actual canal construction.

Some of these are as follows:

1776—General George Washington ordered Thomas Machin to survey a route for a canal across Cape Cod for the purpose of greater security to navigation and to give greater protection against the enemy in time of war.

1791—John Mills and James Winthrop carried out a survey for this same canal.

1808—Secretary Gallatin, United States Treasury, gave his full endorsement to this canal and described it as "useful in time of war."

1818—Isreal Thorndike and Thomas H. Perkins had Loammi Baldwin make a survey for the Canal. Approximately at this time the United States Senate had a survey made for a canal to admit vessels of war.

1860—Surveys for the government reported an 18 foot canal would cost $10,000,000. These surveys were made by Brig. Gen. J. G. Totten, Prof. A. D. Bache, Superintendent Coast and Geodetic survey; Commander C. H. Davis, U.S.N. and Lt. J. Wilkenson, U.S.N.

1870—A charter, the first to be granted to anyone to build a canal, was to Alpheus A. Hardy and others, Cape Cod Ship Canal Company for a sea level canal.

A hydraulic dredge at the east end of the canal at station 70. This type of dredge lowered the bottom of the canal to the opening depth of 18 feet. *Photo courtesy of Ben Harrison, Buzzards Bay.*

Up to 1862, all proposals for a canal were for a lock canal, this thought being caused by the fact that the great difference in height of tides in Cape Cod Bay and Buzzards Bay would cause too great a current for a sea level canal. Further study showed that a sea level canal was the preferred solution. For 10 years - 1870 to 1880 - no work was done by the Cape Cod Ship Canal Company.

In relation to this first charter, the Legislature of Massachusetts passed a resolution that the U. S. Government aid this enterprise by constructing a breakwater at the proposed eastern entrance to the canal. Thereupon, General Foster of the U. S. Army Engineers examined the physical aspects of the project. He found that a canal was possible and practicable and advised favorable on the matter, stating "the line of the canal is the most remarkable piece of physical conformation I have ever seen. Its military value in time of war equals its commercial value in time of peace." In transmitting General Foster's report to the Secretary of War, General A. A. Humphrey (Chief of Engineering) states that breakwaters can be properly classed as a national work and cited the Delaware Breakwater.

Looking west from station 90, on the mainland side of the canal, a large dredge is eating away at the earth. In the background, on the left, is the Keith Car Works, a large manufacturing plant in Sagamore which closed and was torn down in the 1930's. *Photo courtesy of Ben Harrison, Buzzards Bay.*

Similar resolutions by the U. S. Senate and House favored the Government constructing the breakwater and harbor of refuge. In February 1877, no work having been done by the Cape Cod Ship Canal Company, the Committee on Harbors was instructed to examine the condition in relation to this company and on Dec. 26, 1877 filed a report to the legislature stating that the Cape Cod Ship Canal Company probably would not build the canal and also said, "In common with many other committees who have been called upon to investigate the subject, this committee is impressed with the great commercial importance of a properly built canal across Cape Cod to the commerce of Boston, no less than to every city and town on Massachusetts Bay and for thirty or forty miles back from the coast."

In 1880 a new charter granted Henry M. Whitney and others under the name of Cape Cod Canal Company, capital $4,000,000, this charter to take effect November 1, 1880 unless prior to that time the Cape Cod Ship Canal Company undertook the construction of the Canal. To save their original charter the Cape Cod Ship Canal Company, one Mr. Dreisbach in particular, imported 500 laborers from Italy, putting them to work with hand shovels and wheel barrows. This venture failed after a few hundred cubic yards of material, and State authorities removed the Italian laborers and the Whitney charter became operative. In 1881, Whitney surveyed and decided to relinquish. In 1883, William Seward, Jr. and others reorganized the Cape Cod Ship Canal Company and a Frank A. Lockwood, assisted financially by Quincy A. Shaw, built a dredge known as the *LOCKWOOD DREDGE*, floated it in Scusset Creek, Town of Sandwich, and dug only a few hundred thousand cubic yards of material. This company spent approximately $1,500,000 in dredging, building wharves, and settling land damage claims. This project failed and March 22, 1890 the Company was forced to make an assignment to Thomas L. Livermore as trustee for Mr. Shaw. The charter lapsed. Another charter was granted to Alfred D. Fox and others under the name of Boston, Cape Cod and New York Canal Company, nothing was done and the charter lapsed.

LEFT ABOVE: The Dredge *NAHANT* of the Eastern Dredging Company at the east end of the canal opening up the entrance with the material barges just off shore. BELOW: The old draw bridge at Bourne with the Thomas A. Scott Co. dredge *WARFIELD* working beyond. Further down is the old railroad bridge. *Photos courtesy of Ben Harrison, Buzzards Bay.*

On March 31, 1891, Charles F. Chamberlayne, Esq., Council of the town of Bourne, stated before the Commission on Harbors and Public Lands, Washington, D. C. a few grievances of the local citizenry.

"Our enthusiasm for a canal has been much tempered by sad experience. We are heartily sick and tired of irresponsible, absurd mis-management of a scheme of national importance. We are nauseated with stock-jobbing and thimble-rigging pretenses. For twenty years our lands taken by eminent domain have been tied up in court, etc." A further quote: "In 1883 when a new company was organized and at least $25,000 was to be expended in actual construction within four months another farce was enacted. Nothing done until the last moment, then pile drivers built a wharf where there was no harbor and a dredge dug a few feet. In 1887 this charter was extended for four years and now (1891) another extension is asked for. If any of these parties can and will build a canal we want them to have a charter, if not we ask that no charter be granted nor extension be granted. If a canal is to be built, then let it be built. If not, then free our lands from this incubus. After twenty years we think ourselves entitled to this poor indulgence."

With these and other pertinent statements this address no doubt made a profound impression upon the commissions.

On June 1, 1899, Dewitt C. Flanagan and others obtained a charter under the name of Boston, Cape Cod and New York Canal Company and it was under this charter that the canal was built. Five years passed, in 1904 the company was able to interest August Belmont, a financier of note, and immediately progress was made.

TOP: Looking east from station 160 on the mainland side of the canal, situated on a high hill, affords a long view of the eastern end of the canal. The Sagamore draw bridge can be seen in the distance. ABOVE: This is a view of the old Bourne draw bridge. *Photos courtesy of Ben Harrison, Buzzards Bay.*

In 1907, permission was granted them to proceed constructing a canal 100 feet wide on the bottom and 25 feet deep at mean low water. On June 22, 1909, work of digging was begun officially. On July 29, 1914, the Cape Cod Canal was opened, a toll waterway.

The canal was granted permission to open for traffic before the charter depth of 25 feet was reached. The controlling depth was 18 feet when the canal opened in 1914 and the charter depth of 25 feet was completed May 16, 1916 and at this time 15,000,000 cubic yards of material had been removed and the cost to the company was $16,131,000.

On January 25, 1918 the canal was declared completed by the Waterways and Public Lands Commission of Massachusetts. Negotiations by the U. S. Government to buy the canal failed, but it was taken over during World War I and operated by the U. S. Railroad Administration.

ABOVE: The big day was July 29, 1914. The official opening of the Cape Cod Canal began with a flotilla of ships passing through to celebrate the occasion. This is the *ROSE STANDISH*, the second boat in the parade. She followed the *SCOUT* which belonged to Commodore August Belmont. She was, in turn, followed by Navy Craft, Revenue cutters, the boats of prominent citizens and by Police boats. BELOW: At station 160 on the mainland side looking east on opening day with the parade of boats in the flotilla passing through the canal. *Photos courtesy of Ben Harrison, Buzzards Bay.*

Offers of up to $10,500,000.00 by the Government were refused and in March 1920 the canal was returned to the Boston, Cape Cod and New York Canal Company "to operate for the United States Government" until such time as the Federal Courts would decide the purchase price.

On March 31, 1928 the Government took over the canal, and paid $11,500,000.00 for it and the Corps of Engineers, U. S. Army took over the operation. Up to this time the canal had been a toll waterway, but upon Government acquisition, became toll free.

The steamer *BOSTON*, from New York through the Canal creates a beautiful reflection for the photographer on a calm day. *Photo by Fred Small, courtesy of Bourne Historical Society.* BELOW: Tug and barges clearing the west end of the canal. This shot depicts the ultimate motive for the canal. By avoiding the passage around the Cape, this type of commerce had a much safer run between the northern and southern ports. Fewer wrecks on the backside brought higher profits and lower insurance rates for shipowners using the canal. *Photo courtesy of Ben Harrison, Buzzards Bay.*

From March 31, 1928 until 1932, necessary plans and surveys were made and from 1932 to 1935 the canal was dredged to a width of 170 feet on the bottom with controlling depth still 25 feet at mean low water. During this period, three new bridges were built and the old bridges removed. The two high level highway bridges have a vertical clearance at mean high water of 135 feet. The railroad bridge at Buzzards Bay near the west end of the canal's land cut has a vertical lift span of 544 feet, which was the longest of its type in the world until exceeded only recently by a bridge erected between New Jersey and Staten Island, New York. This railroad bridge at the Cape Cod Canal has a vertical clearance, when raised, of 135 feet at mean high water and a horizontal clearance of 466 feet.

103

ABOVE: Photograph taken in 1933 shows the construction of the new Bourne Bridge. *Photo by Fred Small, courtesy of Bourne Historical Society.* BELOW: Widening and dredging of the canal to bring it up to modern requirements in 1935. *Photo courtesy of Ben Harrison, Buzzards Bay.*

From 1935 to 1940 much was accomplished. The channel was widened to 480 feet on the bottom between the eastern entrance and the State Pier at Buzzards Bay, known as the "land cut". A new channel 540 feet on the bottom was dug from the State Pier, out four miles to a point approximately one mile north of Wing's Neck, Pocasset, and the old western approach channel was closed off by a dike between Hog Island and the mainland. This dike being extended to also join Mashnee Island to Hog Island and the mainland of Gray Gables, Bourne, Massachusetts.

Also during this period, a new channel, 700 feet in width, 32 feet deep and approximately four miles long extended the 540 foot Stony Point channel out to Cleveland Ledge Lighthouse in Buzzards Bay, so that a canal 17.4 miles in length with a controlling depth of 32 feet at mean low water became operative in 1940. To this date, a total of 54,000,000 cubic yards of material had been removed to make the Cape Cod Canal what it is today.

Benjamin S. Harrison.

There are some tricky currents that plague pilots on the Cape Cod Canal. The result of a side current is graphically illustrated in the above photograph. The Eastern Steamship Lines *BELFAST*, one of the famous Metropolitan Liners is fast under the Sagamore Bridge, April 16, 1919. *Photo by Small, Buzzards Bay.*

The normal flow of traffic in the canal was interrupted on April 16, 1919 when the Metropolitan Liner *BELFAST* collided with the Sagamore Bridge at ten minutes before six in the morning. The heavy steel girders of the bridge demolished the upper forward decks of the steamer and injured three people.

Side view of the Steamer *BELFAST*. Extensive damage was done to the ship and they had to wait until low tide to move it. *Photo by Small, Buzzards Bay.*

The ship had left New York at 5 P.M. the previous evening and was making a normal run to Boston with a quartermaster at the wheel and the Captain in the pilot house. There was a brisk wind and an easterly current and the ship sheered out of the channel and smashed into the bridge.

The position of the ship prevented the closing of the drawbridge and other vessels from passing through the canal. All vehicle traffic had to use the Bourne bridge.

When the accident happened the Captain and the quartermaster had to leap from the pilot house for their lives. The quartermaster was injured in the mishap as were two passengers in staterooms that were reduced to splinters. When the ship hit the bridge it carried away some twenty feet of the forward superstructure. Mr. E. O. Reed in stateroom 52 suffered broken ribs and other passengers suffered nervous shocks.

The Captain kept a cool head during the disaster and after sending the walking wounded ashore for medical attention he ordered breakfast served for the more than 200 people aboard the *BELFAST*. After a hearty meal, the passengers were taken by tugs and canal service boats to the railroad station in Buzzards Bay and placed aboard a train headed for Boston. Most of them arrived about an hour later than the scheduled arrival time for the steamer.

The ship stayed under the bridge through one complete tide change and the rising tide bent the rails of the forward deck over double. Tugs removed the ship later and towed her to Boston for repairs.

TOP: Eastern Steamship Lines' *NEW YORK* aground in Cape Cod Canal on April 14, 1928. An exceptionally strong westerly tide caused the vessel to go aground. The ship was ashore for 18 hours. ABOVE: Steamer *NEW YORK* listed over at low tide completely blocking the narrow canal. *Photos by Ben Harrison, Buzzards Bay, Mass.*

Another Eastern Steamship Liner blocked the canal a few years later when the *NEW YORK* ran aground at the eastern end of the canal with 491 passengers on board. The ship was headed west toward New York City at the time of the accident. The liner struck on a sand bar about a half mile east of the Sagamore Bridge. The grounding occurred at night when the man at the wheel failed to allow sufficient leeway in steering the craft against a stiff wind and fast moving current. The tide dropped and the huge ship listed to her starboard side completely blocking the waterway to traffic.

The passengers were taken off by a group of local fishing boats and landed in Sandwich. From there they traveled by busses to New London, Connecticut and thence by train to New York City.

The narrow passage in the canal required constant attention on the helm for larger ships when they passed through. It was mishaps such as this that led to a wider and deeper canal. Five years after this accident, work was begun to improve the waterway.

This spectacular aerial photograph by Ben Harrison, taken in August of 1960, shows the canal and Buzzards Bay to Cuttyhunk and Gay Head on the left. The large black area to the right of the canal in the foreground is the parking lot at Scusset Beach and on the left is the village of Sandwich. *Photo by Ben Harrison, Buzzards Bay.*

In addition to a functional waterway, the Cape Cod Canal is also a beautifully scenic place where the public areas permit camping and picnicking. The sport fishing in the canal is reported to be the best on the East Coast. The canal has proven its worth to the economy of the country as a whole and an inestimable contribution during wartime.

During World War II, as many as 70 ships a day passed through to re-group in Cape Cod Bay for the convoys to England, France and Russia. If these ships had been forced to go out and around Cape Cod from their New York departure many would have been lost to the German submarine wolf-packs that plagued the coastline.

The waterway saves from 65 to 150 miles for ships bound north or south between New York and Boston and other east coast ports from the Maritimes to Florida. Approximately 32,000 vessels of all types use this canal annually (including small craft) with approximately 13,360,000 tons of cargo, principally petroleum products.

The canal is open for two-way traffic 24 hours a day, 365 days a year unless fog or accidents cause a closing. Mooring basins on each end provide snug harbors for smaller vessels if needed. Annual dredging by the Corps of Engineers to remove shoals amounts to almost 350,000 cubic yards each year.

Further improvements for canal transit have been installed in the 1970's with closed circuit television cameras installed over the length of the canal and with radar covering both approaches. This will insure safer operations in the future and prevent accidents where they can be prevented.

ABOVE: Sailing ships still ply the waters around Cape Cod. This is the Portuguese training ship *SAGRES* as she passed through the Canal under auxiliary diesel power with her masts housed to clear the bridges. 1972. *Photo by Barbara Russell, Sandwich.* BELOW: Modern day traffic in Cape Cod Canal. The *CUNARD AMBASSADOR* sails through the Canal and sets a pretty picture as she clears the Bourne Bridge. May 1973. *Photo by Quinn.*

ABOVE: The tug *PERTH AMBOY* on the right still afire and the barge *LANSFORD*, sunk on the left of the assistance tug, three miles east of Orleans. Wreckage left by German U-boat attack on tug and four barges on July 21, 1918. BELOW: Survivors from barges sunk by shelling from German U-boat reach Nauset Beach. *Reproduced from photographs loaned by a friend.*

# CHAPTER 7

**World War I and the German sub attack on Cape Cod in 1918.
The rum runners and the submarine disasters on
the Cape during the roaring 20's.**

ABOVE: Barge *LANSFORD*, New York, sunk by shell fire from *U-156* of the Imperial German Navy on July 21, 1918 off Nauset Beach, Orleans. *Reproduced from a photo loaned by The Orleans Yacht Club.*

On Sunday July 21, 1918 the weather was sunny on Cape Cod with a low fog bank just offshore. World War I was tilting back to the allies side and the Imperial Germans were on the defensive. In Orleans, on Cape Cod, people were going to church and the tug *PERTH AMBOY* with Captain Joe Tapley, his wife and 15 crewmen, towing four barges, was gliding along on a glassy sea off the backside of Cape Cod near Nauset Beach. A serene, peaceable scene.

Late in the morning a periscope broke the calm surface of the Atlantic three miles off shore and the *U-156*, a large submarine, belonging to the Imperial German Navy, surfaced and started shelling the tug and her four barges. A well placed shell blasted the wheel house right off the top of the tug and another shell set her on fire. When the four barges were sunk, the sub then lobbed a few shells shoreward and took off, underwater, and left, never to be seen again.

ABOVE: Survivors in boat being helped ashore on Nauset Beach in Orleans following sub attack on tug and barges three miles east of Orleans on July 21, 1918. BELOW: An Orleans lad dons a life jacket from the tug *PERTH AMBOY* and poses for a memorable photograph beside one of the lifeboats on the beach. *Photos loaned by the Orleans Yacht Club.*

Crew of the Tug *PERTH AMBOY* as they appeared on the day following the German Submarine attack. Photo taken at the Orleans Coast Guard Station, July 22, 1918.

Perhaps, if no one had seen the battle save the few survivors from the tug and barges and the men of the Orleans Coast Guard station some six miles from the spot of the shelling, the story would end there. The firing so close to shore, brought out hundreds of people to the beach to see the Hun at work. History was written that day and the story has many witnesses. Orleans churches emptied out their flocks of faithful and the flocks hurried to the beach in their "Model T's" to see the action.

The telephones were busy. On the high bluff overlooking Nauset Beach, Dr. J. Danforth Taylor was on long distance to the Boston Globe, giving a blow by blow description to that newspaper. There were literally hundreds of eyewitnesses to the attack on a defenseless vessel in the territorial waters of the United States. This factor would normally be welcomed by history writers and investigators to the incident. However, years later, eyewitnesses differ as to what did happen that day.

The eyewitnesses had conflicting reports as to whether there was only one or maybe two submarines. The length of the battle was another disputed point. Did the Hun shell the cottages on the beach proudly displaying the American flag or was it just bad shooting? Did the Navy planes from the nearby Chatham Air Station drop dud bombs or as reported, toss a monkey wrench at the departing Germans? The Air Station had just been completed, at a cost of two million dollars, to defend the shores against submarine attack.

The facts bear out some, but not all, of the eyewitness claims. The incident marked the first time that an American ship had been attacked in American waters by an enemy ship of war since the war of 1812. The shells that fell on the beach and marsh behind the beach were the first enemy shells to hit American soil since that same war and it was the first air-sea engagement on this side of the Atlantic in this country's history.

On the day following the attack, the Boston Globe published a cartoon lampooning the event. *From the Boston Globe of July 22, 1918.*

The sub was firing three and four inch shells into the tug and barges. The tug *PERTH AMBOY* was 138 feet long and displaced 452 gross tons, the barges varied in length from 160 feet to 187 feet long, and all had crews. No fatalities were reported, however there were some injuries to tug and barge crews of which 31 were landed on the beach in Orleans including three women and five children. It was generally agreed that the firing lasted about 35 minutes and in that time the only opposition the Germans had was a boy on the deck of one of the barges waving an American flag and two planes from the Chatham air base dropping some dud bombs and/or a monkey wrench. It seems that most of the crew from the air station were in Provincetown that morning for a baseball game and the man with the key to the bomb fuse locker was the catcher for the game.

The German Captain must have been amused at the poor showing by the Americans knowing the proximity of the Chatham Air Station. The Coastguardsmen from the Orleans station assisted the crew of the tug ashore and quartered them at the station. Members of the crews of the barges landed further up the beach towards the town and were taken in and aided by the cottage dwellers on the beach. The next day, they were all transported to the local train station and left for Boston.

The aftermath of the attack was headlines in all of the newspapers and demands for investigations into the reasons why the submarine was not sunk by the Chatham Navy boys. Time cured results and the incident was forgotten except for the historical aspects. Most of the crews went back to sea and the *PERTH AMBOY* was towed to New York City and refitted and went back into service. The day following the attack the barge *LANSFORD*, with her stern still out of water, sank. The barges are still there today and can be seen by skin divers, and now and then foul the nets of fishing trawlers. The exact location is Latitude 41-47-56 North and Longitude 69-52-36 West.

Deck view of the *PERTH AMBOY*, taken in Vineyard Haven, after the attack shows extensive damage to the tug from the shelling and fire.

Some of the names that time has forgotten - Kapitan-Lieutenant Von Oldenberg, skipper of the *U-156*, Captain Joe Tapley of the tug *PERTH AMBOY*, Captain Charles Ainsleigh-barge *LANSFORD*, Captain Harry Rabe-*BARGE #766*, Captain Peter B. Peterson-*BARGE #703*, Captain Joseph Jerry-*BARGE # 740*. Tug and barges owned by the Lehigh Valley railroad, estimated loss was one million dollars. Coast Guard station # 40 on Pochet Island, Captain Robert Pierce, men under his command were William Moore, Elroy Penniman, Allen Gill all of Orleans, Ralph Cook of Wellfleet and Elmore Kenrick of Dennis and in 1973, the only surviving member, living in Orleans is Reuben Hopkins. Fate of the sub was that it hit a mine while returning to base in Germany and sank. Of the 30 crewmen, 21 reportedly made it ashore. The sub was 213 feet long and was the standard long-range type and supported two deck guns and had torpedoes.

The torpedoes were not used in the Orleans shelling, however, one report from a barge crewman said that he saw the sub fire three torpedoes at the barges before surfacing. These have never been found and it would seem that they would end up on the shore had they been fired. No U-boat commander worth his salt is going to waste expensive torpedoes on wooden barges that can be sunk with deck guns.

The official report from the Navy was that everything was done at the time that could be done. About the only big losers in the whole affair was the Lehigh Valley Railroad and the Imperial German Navy. The railroad lost a million dollars in damage to the tug and the sunken barges. The German Navy lost some credibility in that it took some fifty to one hundred shots to sink the four barges that were sitting ducks, and they failed to sink the tug, just set it afire. The winners in the event were the residents of Orleans, witness to a memorable occasion, right on their front doorstep. History was written on the beach in Orleans that day and the people watching it can still recall it and relate the events just as they happened.

Note:   On July 14, 1968 at a regular meeting of the Orleans Historical Society, a discussion was held, along with photographs of the German sub attack on Orleans in 1918. Eyewitnesses told of watching the entire event. The incident was recorded and excerpts are quoted direct from the tape recording. Photographs shown here were taken on July 21, 1918 and loaned by the Orleans Yacht Club and Reuben Hopkins.

The remains of the *LAURA A. BARNES* wrecked on Cape Hatteras in 1921, 4½ miles south of Whalebone Junction. This wreck is one of the biggest tourist attractions in the North Carolina seashore. *Photo by Quinn.*

Cape Cod has been referred to as the "Graveyard of the Atlantic," however, our neighbors to the south claim that morbid distinction. Cape Hatteras, a chain of barrier islands that stretch from Virginia Beach to Morehead City make up the Cape Hatteras National Seashore area where in the early days, legends tell us, pirates roamed these shores. Mooncussers plied their trade and tales of buried treasures still awe the youngsters. A thousand ships have met their fate here.

Cape Hatteras is very similar to Cape Cod, some areas are so alike that one cannot tell the difference when looking at photographs taken in the dune areas. At Cape Hatteras, storms and fog and the wars have piled up a terrible toll of shipwrecks. In 1862 the Federal Ironclad *MONITOR* was sunk off Hatteras in a gale. Many ships were sunk off here in World War I. In 1942, German submarines turned the waters around Cape Hatteras into what was known as Torpedo Junction. Residents can tell stories of seeing as many as five ships burning at once off shore during the war.

There are many shipwrecks here and many tales of heroic deeds by the early Lifesavers. The men here were one up on their Cape Cod brothers in that many of them used to patrol the beaches on horseback. There is evidence on the beaches of bygone shipwrecks. Most picturesque is the wreck of the *LAURA A. BARNES*, near Whalebone Junction, one of the biggest tourist attractions in the seashore.

Perhaps the most notorious distinction is down on Ocracoke Island where Blackbeard the pirate held forth in the early 1700's. They even have historical markers in Ocracoke telling the story of Blackbeard, while on Cape Cod we only have the lesser known Captain Bellamy and his pirate ship *WHIDAH*, which was wrecked in Wellfleet in 1717.

A complete story about Cape Hatteras and her shipwrecks is in the book "Graveyard of the Atlantic", by David Stick.

RIGHT: Peaked Hill Bars stretches for miles around the backside of Provincetown. Hundreds of ships are buried here. *Reproduced from Chart No. 1208.* BELOW: The English steamer *THISTLEMORE* aground on Peaked Hill Bars Feb. 7, 1922. Capt. Emanuel Gracie of the Peaked Hill Coast Guard Station and his crew with the breeches buoy set up ready to bring ashore members of the crew of the *THISTLEMORE. Photo courtesy of Cyril Patrick, Provincetown.* BOTTOM: The crew of the Peaked Hill Coast Guard Station land a member of the crew of the grounded freighter. *Photo courtesy of Cyril Patrick, Provincetown.*

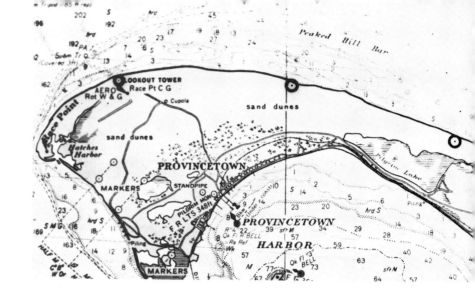

The avid collector of shipwreck photographs will note that the rarest shots to find are the ones of breeches buoy rescues on the beach by the old Lifesavers or the more modern Coast Guard, which are taken during the actual rescue. The four photographs of the British ship *THISTLEMORE* were found in Provincetown by Mr. Cyril Patrick.

TOP: Capt. Emanuel Gracie (back to) aids crewman landing in the surf. Just offshore is C. G. Cutter *OSSIPEE*. BELOW: Capt. Gracie aids another seaman landing in breeches buoy from stricken English freighter *THISTLEMORE* on Peaked Hill Bars, Feb. 7, 1922. *Photos courtesy of Cyril Patrick, Provincetown.*

The *THISTLEMORE* was battling a northeast gale when she came aground on Peaked Hill Bars, 100 yards from shore on February 7, 1922 carrying a crew of 44 men. Capt. Emanuel Gracie of the Peaked Hill Bars station set up the beach apparatus and landed 25 men off the grounded freighter.

Twenty-three men returned to the ship later and on February 12, wrecking tugs managed to free the grounded ship from the shoals. Assistance was rendered at the scene by the Coast Guard cutters *OSSIPEE* and *TAMPA*.

# PROHIBITION PRESTIDIGITATION

The wreck of the *ANNIE L. SPINDLER* is a two part story. Both parts must be taken equally, with drops of salt water, in order to digest and filter out the truth. The first part deals with the trauma of being shipwrecked in a storm, hardship and suffering. The second part deals with chicanery and shenanigans which were unparalled in any other Cape wreck.

On December 29, 1922, as reported in the New Bedford Times, a blizzard was raging and all along the coast a sharp lookout was maintained by the Coast Guard for vessels in distress. A fishing schooner from Nova Scotia came ashore in the breakers in front of the Race Point Coast Guard station in Provincetown. The crew of six had been lashed in the rigging for hours and were in poor condition when removed from their vessel by the Coast Guard using the breeches buoy. The *ANNIE L. SPINDLER* was laden with 800 cases of whisky. No mention of the illegal liquids was made in the newspaper. However, another report from Provincetown tells a different story. . . . . . . . . .

The *ANNIE L. SPINDLER*, British rum runner ashore at Race Point in Provincetown during a northeast gale with 800 cases of good whisky aboard. *Photo courtesy of Cyril Patrick, Provincetown.*

The derelict hull of the *ANNIE L. SPINDLER*, sanded in on the beach in front of the Race Point Coast Guard Station, after it was stripped of all usable equipment. *Photo courtesy of Cyril Patrick, Provincetown.*

The two masted schooner *ANNIE L. SPINDLER* came ashore in Provincetown at Race Point early in the morning of December 29, 1922. The schooner was laden with 800 cases of whisky.

Official records have been (lost?) (hidden?) away to cover up the bungled incident, however an eye-witness from Provincetown relates that 100 cases of the booze was jettisonned just before the vessel went aground.

700 cases were taken off the boat and stored in a warehouse near the Coast Guard station.

Two weeks later the remaining 600 cases were transferred to another warehouse in downtown Provincetown for safe keeping until it could be shipped to Boston.

A few nights later, townspeople raided the warehouse and made off with another 500 cases of the valuable liquids.

A few days later 50 cases of the original 800 were shipped to Boston from Provincetown. This is somewhat of a poor showing so it is no wonder that the records are (lost?) (hidden?) somewhere in the archives.

Officials conducted a house to house search throughout Provincetown for the whisky, and the suspected raiders, but none was found. Our anonymous but reliable eye-witness claimed at the time to have five cases of the stuff hanging by a rope in his cistern. The only other information that the eye-witness would relate was that it was "damn good whisky."

The *ANNIE L. SPINDLER* remained on the beach and was soon stripped by the Provincetown wreckers. She then started to go to pieces. Her hull, however, remained intact and became an attraction for a few years as a picnic site. One night some over-zealous lads from Provincetown burned the hull for a bonfire.

UP FROM THE DEEP
—This was the submarine S-19 pictured ashore at Nauset Beach, Orleans. Waves many feet high were breaking that day and nobody could get near her. This Leslie Jones photo (above) was made from shore with 17-inch lens.

ABOVE: Newspaper photograph and report on the *S-19*, ashore at Eastham, January 15, 1925. BELOW: Submarine *S-19* ashore at low tide, Jan. 1925. *Copied from photo loaned by Russell Taylor, Orleans.*

Another incident with the Coast Guard that paralled the Monomoy Disaster but without the loss of life was the grounding of the *S-19* on Nauset Bar in Eastham. Early in the morning of January 15, 1925, the telephone rang at the Nauset Coast Guard station in Eastham. Captain Abbott H. Walker received notice that a Navy submarine was aground five miles north of the station. The crew could not locate the craft and after daylight came, it was found five miles south of the station near Nauset Inlet aground in heavy seas. Every wave, crashing against the sub erupted into a mountain of spray, hiding the sub from view.

Captain Walker went to the beach with his crew; Henry Daniels, Wilbur Chase, William Eldredge, Kenneth Young and Russell Taylor, and launched the lifeboat in the surf and started to row out to the sub. When within 50 yards of the sub, a giant wave hit the bow of the lifeboat and pitchpoled it over, spilling all of the men into the frigid waters of the Atlantic, smashing the bow of the boat.

All hands, in their heavy rigging of oilskins and rubber boots, managed to hang onto the overturned boat and work their way back to shore where other Coast Guardsmen from the Cahoon's Hollow station had come up to assist the Nauset Crew. They managed to reach a hunting camp on the beach where some townspeople, who had been watching the rescue effort from the opposite shore, came over to help the men warm up from their frigid mishap.

121

News photograph taken two days after the accident with Coast Guardsmen and the boat. This is not the entire crew of the overturned boat. L. to R.: Charles E. Lee, Zenias J. Adams, Yngve Rongner, Bill Eldredge, Henry Daniels and Capt. Walker. Lee, Rongner and Adams were not in the boat when it overturned. *Photo courtesy of Russell Taylor, Orleans.*

The Nauset crew all survived the ordeal but it was a close call for some. The crew of the submarine were subsequently removed. The sub, however, lay on Nauset Bar for three months before it could be removed.

Authentic details about shipwrecks are difficult and sometimes impossible to find. In reporting an incident of shipwreck, no better source can be found than the log of the ship. The Coast Guard cutter *MORRILL* came aground in Provincetown on November 16, 1926 during a southeast gale. The following are entries from the log of the *MORRILL* covering the grounding and subsequent floating, three days later:

11/16 9:00 A.M. to 4:00 P.M. Fresh breeze to fresh Southerly gale, sky partly cloudy.
4:00 P.M. to 8:00 P.M. Fresh increasing to whole Southerly gale and stormy, Very rough sea, 6:00 Ship dragging, appeared to have lost starboard anchor, let go port anchor with thirty fathoms of chain, anchor failed to hold.
6:02 Full speed ahead unable to raise anchor due to strain, Vessel broad side to gale, unable to bring head into wind, Vessel still dragging in spite of fact of engine full ahead and anchor down. 6:10 as order was given to ship anchor, ship grounded, rendering rudder useless, stopped engine, belayed order to ship anchor, due to heavy seas, Vessel was washed inshore bow striking Picketts fish wharf where four bow lines were put out in an attempt to keep head up, two of the bow lines parted and the other two pulled out pilings at end of wharf, it was impossible to put out more lines as the ships bow was gradually carrying away the whole dock, the dock being very old and rotten. This dock is lightly constructed, very weak and has not been in use of late, thus being unable to keep bow up, Vessel continued to be washed further in shore until vessel's quarter fetched up alongside small pavillion dock practically demolishing same due to the continuous heavy sea and gale. Ship aground at Provincetown, Mass., and so ends watch.

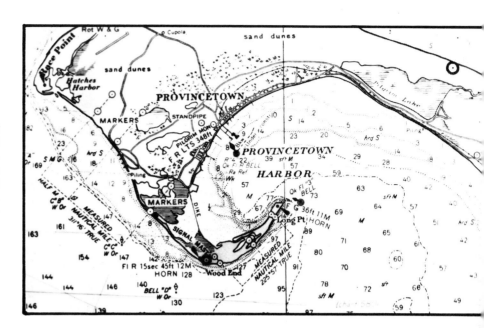

RIGHT: Provincetown Harbor situated at the tip of Cape Cod is a good deep water anchorage. *Reproduced from Chart 1208.* BELOW: USCG Cutter *MORRILL* ashore at Provincetown. Nov. 1926. *MORRILL* was removed from shore three days after the storm that stranded her by the Cutters *OSSIPEE* and *ACUSHNET*. *Photo by L. M. Snow from John Bell Collection, Provincetown.*

An inspection of the hull showed no damage and plans were made to try to float the ship on the next high tide with the assistance of the Destroyer *BARROWS* which was anchored in Provincetown harbor at the time. High tide was at 8:52 A.M. but the destroyer could not get close enough in shore to pass the hawser and the *MORRILL* remained ashore with a watch on the deck and on the shore.

Stern view of U.S.C.G.C. *MORRILL* ashore at Provincetown on Nov. 17, 1926. Ship was removed three days later. *Photo by L. M. Snow — from John Bell Collection, Provincetown, Mass.*

That afternoon the cutters *ACUSHNET* and *OSSIPEE* entered the harbor to take up the job of refloating the *MORRILL* and the log tells of meetings of the Commanding Officers for planning of operations for refloating. The last entry in the log for November 17 is: the authorized number of rations for the number in general mess is 39.

11/18   4:00 A.M. to 8:00 A.M. E'ly airs, and clear weather. Vessel aground, the tide flooding. Officers watch and guard on shore maintained throughout watch. 7:00 *OSSIPEE* changed anchorage to position for pulling, 7:40 *C.G. 2339* picket boat from Wood End station ran hawser from *OSSIPEE* to *MORRILL*, line fast and all ready at 8:00 and so ends watch.

8:00 A.M. to 4:00 P.M. Light S'wly airs to E'sly breeze, clear to cloudy, 8:37 first strain on hawser and commenced pulling. 8:50 — 8" hawser of *MORRILL* parted, using bitter end on each quarter to pulling hawser. 9:17 picket boat ran 10 inch hawser aboard. 9:24 hawser fast and started pulling. 9:30 working engine to bells. 9:40 Vessel moved a few feet — stern moving offshore. 10:20 Cast off hawser, orders of Senior Officer, tide having dropped about 1½ feet. Vessel moved with pulling, leaving same in favorable position for pulling with stern about 60 ft. off shore. 1:05 Commanding Officer went aboard *ACUSHNET* for conference.

The remainder of the day was spent taking precautions for preparations for the next days pulling. Friday the 19th started with a fresh E'ly breeze with overcast and rainy weather. The *OSSIPEE* changed anchorage at 8:35 in a position for pulling and the picket boat *C.G.2339* again ran the hawser from *OSSIPEE* to *MORRILL* and it was made fast at 9:00 A.M. The watch changed at 9:00 A.M. and the entry in the log states:

9:00 A.M. to 4:00 P.M. Fresh S'Ely breeze to light westerly breeze. Sky partly cloudy. Weather clear.

9:20 Cutter *OSSIPEE* and *ACUSHNET* started to pull on *MORRILL*.

9:23 Vessel started to move. 9:25 Vessel afloat all clear.

9:25 Sounded bilges and found to be dry. 9:53 Let go hawser and proceeded towards railroad dock under own steam. 10:05 Moored to Railroad dock, Provincetown, Mass.

The next day the *MORRILL* proceeded to Boston and stayed there for a few months and was noted in late December to enter Boston Navy Yard.

During the first world war the *MORRILL* was on duty with the U.S. Navy and on a voyage from Detroit, Michigan to Philadelphia she called at Halifax, Nova Scotia on December 5, 1917. There was no dock space available so the *MORRILL* anchored across the harbor near Dartmouth Cove to replenish her fuel and water. The events of the next 24 hours are now history.

The old freighter *MONT BLANC* was carrying a load of munitions and was in a collision with the Norwegian ship *IMO*. There was a fire aboard the *MONT BLANC* and shortly afterward she blew up turning the port of Halifax into a mass of ruins causing $35 million in property damage and killing over 1,600 people and injuring 9,000 more. There was no serious damage to the *MORRILL* and a rescue party was sent ashore to aid the injured onshore.

The *MORRILL* was built in 1889 and was in the Revenue Cutter service or in service for the U.S. Navy from 1889 to October 1928 when she was sold out of the service.

On January 2, 1927 at 12:30 a.m., the Boston Fishing boat *A. ROGER HICKEY* hit a sandbar off Wellfleet. Loaded with 20,000 pounds of fish and homeward bound, the vessel was wrecked by a faulty compass. There were fifteen foot seas at the time and Coast Guardsmen from the Cahoon's Hollow station made a gallant effort to save the crew of seven aboard the ill-fated craft.

The *A. ROGER HICKEY* ashore on the Outer Bar, Wellfleet. Seven men were saved by the Coast Guard by breeches buoy in 15 foot waves. Jan. 2, 1927. *Photo courtesy of Cyril Patrick, Provincetown.*

The *A. ROGER HICKEY* was a two year old boat with all the latest equipment for fishing and for the comfort of the men aboard. Electric lights in the crews quarters were a luxury in those days and the crew had been listening to their radio the evening before and Graham McNamee broadcasting the exciting Rose Bowl football game at Pasadena, California. The Crew retired early with their craft making an easy passage home.

Captain John R. Hickey was on watch with his son George. With a jet black sky and low overcast and with low visibility, Captain Hickey made Nauset Lighthouse off Eastham and then set his course by the ship's compass and turned in with orders to be called at 1 o'clock. He was headed for Highland Light, as he thought, but the ship's compass was more than a point off true.

The vessel hit the bar hard and the following surf spun the *HICKEY* around broadside of the waves and then began a five hour battle with the elements to save the crew. At the Cahoon's Hollow station, the lookout spotted the wreck when she hit the bar and called Chief Boatswains Mate Henry O. Daniels who aroused his crew and went to the aid of the vessel.

The Coast Guardsmen tried to launch their surfboat into the fifteen foot waves. Three times the boat was thrown back onto the beach, on the fourth try the men succeeded in getting out through the high surf. The effort was in vain as the huge combers made it impossible to get close enough to the ship to afford a transfer of personnel.

Before long a giant wave tossed the Coast Guard boat back almost onto the beach and the men decided upon a different course of rescue.

Beaching the surfboat, the Coast Guardsmen hurried back to the station and brought back the beach apparatus. Chief Daniels landed the shot in the rigging of the *HICKEY* on the third try. Crewmen aboard the vessel were by this time exhausted from their night long battle with the sea but managed to bring the lines aboard for the breeches buoy and make them fast to the rigging.

Seven men and a dog were brought ashore and the last to leave the ship was her Captain at 6:30 a.m. The crewmen were taken to the station and put to bed, following their ordeal, for some much needed rest. That afternoon the sea began the final destruction of the *A. ROGER HICKEY.* The engine and much of her gear were salvaged but the sea claimed the hull, the schooner broke up within a week.

126

ABOVE: U.S.C.G.C. *PAULDING* CG-17, formerly Navy Destroyer *DD-22. PAULDING* rammed and sank the Navy Submarine *S-4* off Wood End in Provincetown, December 17, 1927 with a loss of all hands aboard the submarine. This was one of the old World War I four stackers that was transferred to the Coast Guard to aid in the battle against rum runners, during prohibition times. *Photo courtesy of Mariners Museum, Newport News, Va.* BELOW: Salvage tug with lines out and pontoons down during *S-4* salvage. *Photo courtesy of Leo Gracie, Provincetown.*

One of the worst marine disasters in modern times occurred late on the afternoon of December 17, 1927. The Coast Guard cutter *PAULDING*, a converted four-stack destroyer was coming around Wood End heading into Provincetown harbor. The Navy submarine *S-4* was running submerged in the deep water toward Herring Cove.

Shortly after 3:30 p.m. the *S-4* started to come to the surface right in the path of the *PAULDING* and the four stacker ran right up on the submarine cutting a huge gash in the conning tower and ripping a 15 foot slice through the *PAULDING*'s port bow. The submarine sank in 100 feet of water. The *PAULDING* with her bow low in the water limped into Provincetown Harbor and the word went out to the world of the tragedy.

ABOVE: Conning tower of Submarine *S-4* with pontoons during salvage operations, Provincetown, Mass. *Photo courtesy of Leo Gracie, Provincetown.* BELOW: After the sub was brought up it was towed to the Boston Navy Yard for repairs at Charlestown, Mass. *Photo courtesy of New Bedford Standard Times.*

The drama that unfolded just after the accident was almost as bad as the collision. Thirty-four men died when the *S-4* went to the bottom, but six men survived in the forward torpedo room and divers down looking at the sub contacted the trapped men by tapping on the side of the hull of the sunken submarine. The men lasted only a few days. In 1927 there were no methods devised yet for the rescue of men trapped aboard a sunken submarine.

It took three months to attach the six big pontoons to the sub and she came to the surface on the afternoon of March 17, 1928. The *S-4* was towed to Boston where it was repaired and refitted. The sub was used after that as an experimental craft devoted to devising greater safety measures for submariners. The lessons learned from the *S-4* tragedy were applied 12 years later in 240 feet of water off New Hampshire when the submarine *SQUALUS* sank off Portsmouth with a crew of 59. Using a diving bell, 33 of the crewmen were saved. Each year, services are conducted in a Provincetown church to pay respects to the memory of the dead of the *S-4*.

128

# CHAPTER 8

**The Last sailing ship wreck on the backside of Cape Cod and
an interview with one survivor. The quiet 30's with few
wrecks on Cape Cod.**

After the canal opened in 1915, the ship traffic along the outer shores began to dwindle. There were long periods of inactivity for the many Coast Guard stations along the backside. Beginning in the early twenties, fewer and fewer sailing vessels would ply the waters of the Atlantic as steam had come of age and most of the three and four masted schooners that had once been the mainstay of commerce, had been retired.

With the passage of the prohibition act, the role of the Coast Guard was transposed from that of the shore to that of the sea. The men in the service had to become law enforcers in addition to life savers, hence there was more action at sea, chasing rum runners, than on the shore handling shipwrecks.

The Coast Guard stations along the outer Cape began to cut down on personnel and some stations closed completely. But the wrecks continued to occur although with less frequency as before. One of the stations that had been reduced in crew size was the Orleans station, and it came at a bad time.

The schooner *MONTCLAIR* was wrecked in March of 1927 on the beach in front of the Orleans station and the man in charge of the station had to call for volunteers to help aid in the rescue of the men aboard the *MONTCLAIR*. Only three men were on duty at the time of the wreck. Had there been a full crew, a complete surfboat crew might have averted the disaster that followed.

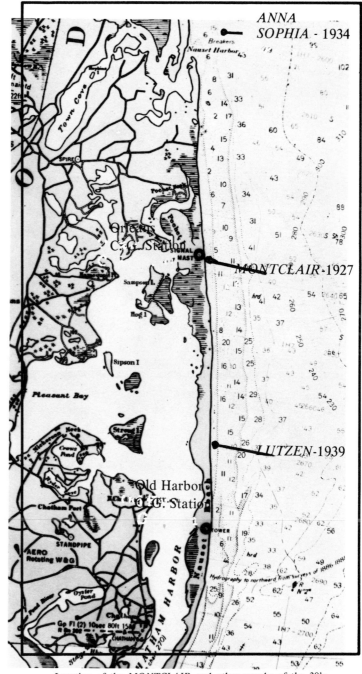

Location of the *MONTCLAIR* and other wrecks of the 30's.
*Reproduced from Chart No. 1208.*

ABOVE: The schooner *MONTCLAIR* wreckage piled high on Nauset Beach in Orleans. The cargo of lath was spread for miles up and down the beach, March 5, 1927. LEFT: Stern section of the *MONTCLAIR* with souvenir hunters picking up mementos and household items. BELOW: View of the bow and stern sections. Five men were lost and the ship a total wreck.

ABOVE: Broken bow section of the schooner *MONTCLAIR* in the surf. RIGHT: Broken stern section of the *MONTCLAIR*. BELOW: The *MONTCLAIR* wreckage 30 years later, March 4, 1957. William P. Quinn Jr., age 3 standing on the port deck aft. The stern section has turned around and was nearly sanded in. This wreckage has now totally disappeared.

Capt. Baggs returns. Mr. & Mrs. Nathan Baggs with Norman Hopkins and Howard Quinn (holding wreck photo) in the parking lot at Nauset Beach, Orleans, September 11, 1968. *Photo by Quinn.*

The events of a shipwreck are best told by the one who has lived through the ordeal. Nathan Baggs returned to Orleans in 1968 to visit the scene of the *MONTCLAIR* wreck. Howard W. Quinn talked with Captain Baggs and this is his story of the wreck of the schooner *MONTCLAIR:*

"We left Halifax March 1st on a clear wintry day early in the morning, with all sails set. We had good sailing until the evening of the second day. Then down off Cape Sable we ran into some dirty weather. The weather continued to get worse during the night. It started to snow, out of the northeast. After this, the storm just seemed to grow worse every hour. We took in all the sails except for the mizzen, and that we had slacked off."

Captain Nathan Baggs, a small weather beaten, slightly bald, with graying hair, but a chipper "young" man in his late sixties, sat on an old wreck on Nauset Beach, in early September 1968 reminiscing about this particular wreck. The details just seemed to flow from his memory of over 40 years age at this very spot. He continues his story. . . . .

"Four days after leaving Halifax, at 5 a.m., we struck the outer bar of Nauset Beach. Oh, we knew where we were all time, but in that northeast gale, with only the mizzen, and that close-reefed, and the vessel was covered with ice, there wasn't much we could do but try and ride out the storm. Then the deck cargo let go, and you couldn't move around much after that. Those lathes just seemed to be every which way, and you couldn't have gone aft from the fo'castle if you had wanted to.

132

Capt. Baggs at the remains of the mid-hull section of the wreck of the *MONTCLAIR* on Nauset Beach, September 11, 1968. The Captain picked up some souvenirs to take back home. *Photo by Quinn.*

"Shortly after she struck the outer bar, we could see men on the beach, then we heard a shot, and saw them trying to shoot a line out to us, but we were too far off shore for them to reach us. About an hour later she started to break up. She cracked just forward of the mizzen and you could see the cargo start floating out of the holds. It had stopped snowing but the surf was still tremendous and the wind was still blowing strong. All of a sudden a big wave hit us and six men were washed overboard. Why I wasn't I will never know. Then I saw the young fellow, Short, and I grabbed him and pulled him back aboard, but the Captain, the Mate, the Cook and the other two were gone. Short and I just hung on to the port quarter rail in the lee of the aft cabin.

"About an hour after the Captain and the rest of the crew were washed overboard the stern of the ship started working in toward the beach with the tide coming in, and finally after many tries, the Coast Guard got a line aboard. I grabbed it, pulling in the slack, tied the line to Short and myself, and the Coast Guard pulled us ashore.

"I don't remember much about that but I do remember they took us to the Coast Guard station, it was about 10:30 a.m., they gave us hot coffee, a rub down, and put us to bed. I think I slept all the rest of that day and into the night. I have never forgotten that day, nor never will."

These are the words of a man who was shipwrecked on Nauset Bar, March 4, 1927 aboard the three masted lumber schooner *MONTCLAIR*. On September 10, 1968 he came back to Nauset Beach. He was then a retired sea captain after 40 years at sea. Capt. Nathan L. Baggs who was born in Newfoundland and was then living in Dartmouth, Nova Scotia, just wanted to come back and see what was left after 40 years. He saw a picture of the wreck of the *MONTCLAIR* in the August 1962 issue of the National Geographic Magazine, and vowed to someday go and see it for himself.

The two survivors of the *MONTCLAIR* Disaster with two Coastguardsmen. Left to Right, Capt. Clark, Garland Short, Nathan Baggs & Surfman John Adams.

"What happened after that? Well I went to Boston then to Parrsboro, Nova Scotia where I gave as much information as I could to the owners in Parrsboro. You see the log was gone and I was the older of two seamen survivors so I had to tell what had happened. While I was there, I visited with the Captain's family and one of the crew's family, then I went home to Halifax. After about two weeks at home, I shipped out again on another schooner for the same company, running from Halifax to New York.

"That afternoon, they found the Captain's body right under the stern. The next day the Coast Guard found two more bodies that came ashore. I think it was just after midnight about two miles down the beach. The next body was found a week later, some five miles south. I don't think they ever did find the last one. I stayed at the Coast Guard Station about two days. They tried their best to get me to stay and sign on, even said they would fix things with immigration and customs, but I wanted to go home."

The destruction of the three masted lumber schooner *MONTCLAIR*, the loss of her skipper, mate and three other men, combined to make the wreck one of the most spectacular ever witnessed on the Cape Cod shoreline. The *MONTCLAIR* was registered in Parrsboro, Nova Scotia, and was four days out of port laden with 25,000 bundles of lath.

The heaviest sea of years was running when Capt. Edward L. Clark of the Orleans Coast Guard sighted the three masted schooner on the bar, a quarter mile from the station. The station, at the time, was in the process of being deactivated and operated with less than the required quota of men. The Captain, surfmen Chase and Adams, were the only ones on duty. These three started at once to launch a boat to go to the distressed schooner. The heavy seas made launching a boat impossible. Time and time again the men made attempts to launch the boat. Time and time again combers rolling in on the beach completely submerged the men. The sea water froze over them almost as it struck. The mercury read fifteen degrees above zero, and a thirty mile northeaster was blowing.

At daybreak, volunteers from Orleans, able seamen with many rescue experiences to their credit arrived to assist the station crew. When it was finally realized it would be impossible to launch a boat, and dawn revealed the plight of the lath laden schooner fast on the bar being pounded by heavy seas, sails frozen beyond use, the Coast Guard crew aided by volunteers, attempted to use the breeches buoy. Meanwhile one volunteer walked five miles to the Old Harbor station for help and another, four miles to the nearest telephone in Orleans to summon aid from the Nauset Coast Guard station in Eastham. The gale had severed all Government beach telephone connections between stations.

Shortly after dawn, those on the beach could see the giant comber coming that resulted in the six men being washed overboard. Moments later they could see the heads of men holding in the water, filled with bundles of laths and parts of the broken schooner. One man was seen trying to lash bundles of laths together with his arms and legs to serve as a raft. Soon the men disappeared from sight being carried with the laths along with the tide. On the stern deck, where seven men were seen a few minutes before, two could now be made out holding on for life against the arrival of still another gigantic wave like the one that had swept five of their shipmates into the raging sea.

Finally the vessel was close enough and the next shot just made the lee rail and it was grabbed by one of the men on the wreck. They saw a wave from the men and the Coast Guards and the volunteers started pulling the line in from the wreck with the two men attached. When the men were brought ashore, one was unconscious and at first thought dead, and the other was on the verge of collapsing and completely exhausted. They hurried the two men to the station where doctors from Orleans were awaiting their arrival and attended them.

Both men recovered and were able to go to Boston by train several days later. The two survivors were Nathan L. Baggs and Garland Short, both born in Newfoundland. The Captain was William McLeod 60, of Parrsboro, N.S. He was survived by a wife, three sons and a daughter. He had been sailing Nova Scotia schooners along the Maritime and New England coasts for more than 35 years. The others were: The mate, William Dowling of Gaborouse, Cape Breton, N.S., ship's cook, Jerome Butler, of St. John, N.B., Seaman William Stuart of Burge, Newfoundland and Seaman George Carns from Newfoundland. All those men lost were married and had families in Canada.

Howard W. Quinn

Note: Numerous photographs of *MONTCLAIR* wreck were loaned by the family of the late Henry O. Daniels of Orleans.

The two masted schooner *ANNA SOPHIA* anchored off Nauset Beach after a storm forced her crew to anchor and leave the ship. The ship did not sink and was restored and went back to sea with her crew of five. *Photo courtesy of Yngve Rongner, Eastham.*

There was a bitter cold snap in the winter of 1934 and huge ice cakes, some 10 feet high were piled up along the Nauset Beach. On Thursday evening, February 8th a squall hit the two masted schooner *ANNA SOPHIA* and carried away her sails and jib boom 10 miles off Race Point.

The 102' vessel was out of New York for Lubec, Maine with 275 tons of coal, a crew of five men and a dog. She drifted down the backside of the Cape and anchored the next morning in sea fog, a mile and a half off Eastham. The ship was heavy with ice and her poles were bare. Only her topmast was visible from the Nauset Coast Guard Station in the low lying fog.

Later in the morning, the fog cleared and the men of the schooner decided to leave the ship and go ashore. They left the ship in the dory and were being swept out to sea by the currents and tide when Boatswains Mate George Nickerson of the Nauset Station ordered out the station lifeboat to go to the aid of the imperiled schooner crew. The boat had to be carried two miles down the beach in order to find an opening in the heavy ice cakes that were piled up the entire length of the beach.

The Coast Guard crew was drenched before they got their lifeboat afloat and on their way to the rescue. The sub zero temperatures froze the clothing of the lifeboat crew making rowing difficult if not impossible. Once clear of the shore, the lifeboat had to battle through the floe ice until they cleared the outer bar.

Coast Guardsmen reached the crew of the schooner and transferred them aboard the

The Nauset Coast Guard crew landing the crew of the *ANNA SOPHIA* on the beach after they left their schooner anchored off shore. *Photo courtesy of Yngve Rongner, Eastham.*

lifeboat and with a hard pull they brought the heavily laden lifeboat back to safety on shore. The crew of the schooner was rushed to the station where a doctor attended to frost-bitten fingers and ears. The ship was later towed to Provincetown by a Coast Guard cutter and fitted out with new sails. The crew was driven to Provincetown and began their journey again under better conditions.

During the era of the speakeasy and into the 1930's there were many stories in the newspapers about G-Men and Coast Guards in running gun fights with rum runners on Cape Cod. Details were sketchy and very little information was given out by the Coast Guard unless the culprits were captured. The smugglers used to keep one step ahead of the authorities however, and usually the stories ended up with the desperadoes escaping in a fast boat.

Legends have been written about the rum runners and many interesting stories have yet to be told. No one talked about it, especially those involved in the illegal dealings. Quick handsome profits were there to be made for those who were cunning and daring. Those with more of the latter and less of the former ended up in jail. During prohibition, whisky was not hard to get, it was just expensive.

One amusing story involved a cod fisherman who made "expense" money on the side by bringing in a few cases of scotch whisky stowed under the codfish catch. On one cold winter trip, he decided to have a little "nip" to combat the icy conditions on board the boat. One "nip" leads to another and our friend was completely three sheets to the wind when other fishermen found him 50 miles from shore headed for Scotland.

The Coast Guard life saving abilities were not limited to the coast lines of the United States. In January of 1937, the mid-western rivers of the country went on the rampage and floods devastated the countryside from Ohio down through Kentucky and beyond. Coast Guard units from Cape Cod with their surfboats went to Ohio to aid flood victims as 400,000 people were homeless in the flood areas.

Forty men and ten surfboats left from Cape Cod in the middle of January and loaded their boats on flatcars in Boston for the train trip across the country. Large portions of Louisville, Kentucky and Cincinnati, Ohio were under water.

137

TOP: The tug *PLYMOUTH* sunk at the east end of the Canal in collision with collier *EVERETT* on January 27, 1938. The barge the tug was towing is tied to piers in background. ABOVE: Divers down on the tug *PLYMOUTH* at the east end of Cape Cod Canal. Engineers control station (with tower) center background. White building (with tower) left background is Coast Guard Station. *Photos courtesy of Army Corps of Engineers.*

On January 27, 1938, a clear evening with no wind and an ebb tide running, the collier *EVERETT* of Boston rammed and sank the tug *PLYMOUTH* at 6:25 p.m. Sixteen members of the crew of the tug were thrown into the icy waters of the Cape Cod Canal. The tug sank three minutes after the collision. The crew had hardly enough time to don life preservers.

The crew tried to stay together in the darkness and swim toward the barge that the tug had been towing. The fast current running in the canal prevented men from reaching the coal laden barge. Following the collision Captain Joseph A. Goodwin, of Orlando, Florida pulled the whistle cord and tied it down. The tug sank to the bottom of the canal sounding a death knell on her whistle. The move was a good one as the noise alerted those on the sides of the canal and immediate action was forthcoming.

Benjamin Harrison, on watch at the east station of the Corps of Engineers control heard the whistle blast and hurried to a motor launch and sped to the scene. Harrison pulled eleven men from the chilly waters of the canal. The Coast Guard station at the east end of the canal brought out two boats and pulled men from the water.

In all fifteen men were rescued and one man was lost. The tug was bound from New York City to Salem, Mass. with the barge full of coal. The barge was secured later to the north side of the canal and the tug was ultimately removed from the bottom of the canal.

In September of 1938, a mammoth hurricane hit New England and did millions of dollars in damage to Rhode Island and Connecticut but Cape Cod escaped most of the worst of the storm. Damage was heavy along the southwestern coastal areas of the Cape but the heavy death toll and millions in damage caused by the storm all occurred west of Cape Cod.

# THE BLUEBERRY BOAT

On February 3, 1939 the 339 ton Canadian freighter *LUTZEN* was lunking along in dense fog when she went aground on North Beach in Chatham in the vicinity of Old Harbor Coast Guard station. The ship did not hit hard and was lying easily in the sand, however, when the crew tried to launch a dory in the surf the boat capsized and one man was lost.

The *LUTZEN* was on her way from St. John N.B. to New York City with 230 tons of frozen blueberries and other mixed cargo when the grounding occurred. Capt. Robert J. Randall of St. John, N.B. said that the entire trip from St. John had been shrouded in fog and that he had looked for Highland and Nauset Lighthouses but could not find them and that they had grounded in pea soup fog at Chatham.

The 135′ freighter sat on the beach for a few days while some attempts were made to pull her off but a northeast storm tossed her high and dry on the sands, so some local laborers were hired at 75 cents per hour to unload the cargo of blueberries from the ship. For some unknown reason, the entire starboard side of the cargo was offloaded onto the beach in one day. The next day the tide tipped the *LUTZEN* over on her port side beam ends and any thoughts at salvage were soon abandoned.

The entire cargo was landed on the beach. The well-being of frozen goods depends a great deal upon the temperature. A warm spell set in and half the cargo was lost. Many of the berries ended up in outer Cape blueberry pies.

The part of the cargo that was saved was transported off the beach into freezer trucks and then to the freezer plant off the Cape. The freighter became a haven for the Cape wreckers and her hull still sits in the water just north of the Old Harbor station and is visible from the air at low tide.

The Canadian Freighter *LUTZEN* with a cargo of blueberries grounded on Nauset Beach near Old Harbor Coast Guard Station, Feb. 3, 1939. The ship came ashore in dense fog. *Photo courtesy of Cape Cod Standard Times.*

ABOVE: Wreckers start to unload the cargo of blueberries. *Photo loaned by Lewis Gill.* LEFT: The crew of the *LUTZEN* are landed ashore by the Old Harbor Coast Guard crew. *Photo by Cape Cod Standard Times, Hyannis.* BELOW: Chief Boatswain Mate Charles R. Ellis (left) on the beach talking with Capt. Robt. J. Randall, Captain of the *LUTZEN*. *Photo courtesy of Cape Cod Standard Times, Hyannis.* BELOW LEFT: Steamer *LUTZEN* on her port side after salvage operations. *Photo courtesy of Y. Rongner, Eastham.* BELOW RIGHT: Salvage operations in progress, hole in hull to remove engines. *Photo courtesy of Y. Rongner, Eastham.*

# CHAPTER 9

**The blocking of the Cape Cod Canal during World War II.**
**Torpedo Junction, the Vineyard Lightship and the Cape Ann.**

Collier *STEPHEN R. JONES* down by the bow in Cape Cod Canal, June 28, 1942. The changing tide caused the *JONES* to veer around and sink broadsides of the canal completely blocking traffic. *Photo courtesy of Corps of Engineers.*

During World War II a collier wreck in the Cape Cod Canal closed the waterway for a month making it necessary for all shipping to go around the backside of the Cape. It was 3 o'clock in the morning on June 28, 1942 and the S.S. *STEPHEN R. JONES* was enroute from Norfolk, Virginia to Boston with 7,149 tons of soft coal. The steamer struck the north bank of the canal 2,000 feet east of the Bourne Bridge and sank by the bow. Later that day when the tide turned in the canal, the stern of the vessel was pushed around by the current and hit the south bank. Later that night the vessel sank almost broadside of the canal.

A multitude of problems arose at once from the accident. Spring tides were running and currents in the canal were at their strongest resulting in serious damage to the slopes on the north and south sides of the canal as the water rushed around either end of the sunken ship. Because the country was at war, danger was increased to vessels having to travel around the Cape and try to elude the German submarines that were cruising just off the coast.

ABOVE: *STEPHEN R. JONES* (stern view) sunk in Cape Cod Canal blocking traffic in the canal. LEFT: Canal engineers explode charges aboard sunken collier *STEPHEN R. JONES* to clear Cape Cod Canal during World War II. It took 28 days to blast the passage clear of the sunken ship loaded with 7,149 tons of coal cargo. *Photos courtesy of Corps of Engineers.*

Because of the many problems, engineers did not delay in correcting the situation. The quickest and most obvious solution was to blow up the hull with explosives. To ease the objections of the local citizens, the engineers began the demolition on July 4th, 1942. No one could object to a little noise on the fourth and the blasting continued for 28 days until the last obstruction in the canal was cleared.

It took 17½ tons of dynamite to complete the job. The largest blast was one of 1,700 lbs., used to blow up the stern section. The surrounding area was uneffected by the explosions although engineers kept a close check on the levels and alignment of the Bourne Highway Bridge after each detonation. Some minor damage to four private homes was reported.

When you pass through the canal in your boat, check the compass, it will swing 360 degrees when you pass over the remains of the *STEPHEN R. JONES* 2,000 feet east of the Bourne highway bridge.

ABOVE: World War II. Torpedoed ship passing through Cape Cod Canal, bow shot away in war action. BELOW: Torpedoed tanker passing through Cape Cod Canal, hole in side of ship below & above waterline. *Photos courtesy of Corps of Engineers.*

During World War II the visible signs of war were brought to the front door of Cape Codders to see almost any day at the Cape Cod Canal. Much of the wartime commerce was the ships moving from the New York area, up to Buzzards Bay, then through the canal and on towards Nova Scotia where the convoys were formed for the trip across the North Atlantic. Some convoys used to make up in Cape Cod Bay. The ships would return on the same route. On these return trips the damage to the ships could be seen from the banks of the canal. Some with huge gaping holes in the side of the hull and one ship, pictured here, with the underside of her bow blown off.

Two way radio traffic was banned during the war because the enemy could monitor the messages of ships passing through the canal and know who and what to expect off shore. The Coast Guard took over the operations of the canal on July 1, 1942 and a pilot and an armed guard were placed aboard each ship that arrived at the entrances and the pilot steered the ship through the canal and got off at the other end. He was rushed back to bring another one through.

William "Sparky" Donovan, a long time dispatcher at Cape Cod Canal headquarters tells about seeing convoys of 70 ships going through the canal, one at a time, and the only way they could be logged was to watch when the ship passed the Coast Guard station and flipped her name board. The board covered up the name of the ship and was lifted to identify the ship as it passed the Coast Guard station while making the passage through the canal. Donovan said that sometimes two or three ships passing in a convoy would have torpedo damage. Raw evidence of war was displayed to the American people here frequently during the hostilities.

The canal was returned to the control of the civilian Army Engineers from the Coast Guard on Sept. 24, 1945.

# THE VINEYARD LIGHTSHIP

Lightship duty around Cape Cod had its ups and downs in years past. As one old timer put it "You were either scared to death or else bored to death." There was more of the latter than the former but on the night of Sept. 14, 1944, a hurricane hit Cape Cod and did four million dollars in property damage and took sixteen lives.

During the height of the storm, residents of Cuttyhunk reported seeing flares fired into the sky near the station of the *VINEYARD LIGHTSHIP*. There was no word in any of the local papers about the tragedy until September 19th when the New Bedford Standard Times reported that the lightship was reported off station and was feared lost. The Navy reported the loss of the ship but the Coast Guard only would report that the lightship was off station.

With the war going on, most news of this sort was sharply curtailed or not reported at all, but the *VINEYARD LIGHTSHIP* contained a local crew and local boys are important. The local papers continued to dig out the true story and finally on Sept. 23rd, the Coast Guard reported that the ship had sunk in the storm and divers had located the hull on the bottom in 60 feet of water lying on her side. The divers reported that the masts and funnels of the ship were broken off flush with the deck but that the mooring chains were still intact and they could find no bodies.

The day after the storm, five bodies washed ashore on Cuttyhunk Island and these were identified as coming from the *VINEYARD LIGHTSHIP*. Five crewmembers were on shore leave at the time of the storm. The twelve men aboard the ship were all lost.

Nineteen years later, divers from the Fairhaven Whalers Diving Club brought up the ship's bell and other items from the sunken hull.

# VINEYARD LIGHTSHIP BELL

This bell, mounted aboard the Vineyard Lightship, once rang to warn ships of dangerous reefs located near the entrances to Buzzards Bay and Vineyard Sound. On September 14, 1944, the Lightship sank at the height of a hurricane with a loss of all 12 men on board.

Nineteen years later, the ship's bell was brought up by the Fairhaven Whalers Diving Club and presented to the Life Saving Museum of Cape Cod National Seashore.

The Sea Gives Up the Bell.

ABOVE: The *VINEYARD LIGHTSHIP* bell plaque with the story of the loss of the lightship. This plaque was used by the Cape Cod National Seashore to display the bell. It has since been moved to an off-Cape museum. *Photo by William P. Quinn.* OPPOSITE: The *VINEYARD LIGHTSHIP*. Hull #73, sunk with all hands during a hurricane in 1944. Wartime photo shows the vessel armed with gun on her stern. *Photo courtesy of U.S. Coast Guard, Washington, D. C.* BELOW: The *VINEYARD LIGHTSHIP* bell. *Photo by William P. Quinn.*

# CAPE ANN ON CAPE COD

On March 6, 1948, the 84 foot New Bedford scallop dragger *CAPE ANN* grounded on Nauset Beach in Eastham at 3:30 a.m., near the Nauset Lighthouse. The vessel had just finished an eleven day fishing trip on Georges Bank and had on board 700 gallons of sea scallops. The crewman at the wheel said that he mistook Nauset Light in Eastham for the *POLLOCK RIP LIGHTSHIP* in Chatham. The *POLLOCK RIP LIGHTSHIP* was stationed six miles southeast of Chatham lighthouse at that time but has since been replaced by a buoy.

There was a heavy swell running at the time and the dragger was badly iced up on deck. Coast Guardsmen from the Nauset Station in Eastham set up the breeches buoy from the top of the bluff and brought five men ashore from the dragger. Captain Alex Nerlind of New Bedford and three other crewmen elected to stay on board the stricken boat to try to save their cargo.

The scene early in the morning was one of despair for the vessel and her crew. Icy waves were breaking over her stern and the heavy surf was breaking up the boat. However, the crew prevailed and early in the afternoon the dragger was high and dry and the crew off-loaded the catch of scallops and they were brought by truck to New Bedford.

The *CAPE ANN* was a total loss as far as the hull was concerned. Most of the deck and fishing gear were salvaged by the crew but the hull went to pieces soon after.

ABOVE: A crowd always gathers on the beach to look at a Cape Cod Shipwreck. Note the lines & breeches buoy on the left-hand side of the photograph. *Photo by Phil Schwind, Eastham.*

RIGHT: Later in the afternoon when the tide dropped people gathered at the wreck. There were 700 gallons of scallops aboard the CAPE ANN which were loaded aboard a Coast Guard truck and taken to New Bedford. *Photo by True Fife, Eastham.*

ABOVE: T-2 tanker *FORT MERCER*, Feb. 18, 1952, 30 miles southwest of Chatham, Mass. broke in half during a Northeast storm. Five men were lost. Tanker stern shown with Coast Guard Cutter *EASTWIND* in foreground. Coast Guard tug *ACUSHNET*, upper left. BELOW: The lifeboat from the Coast Guard Cutter *YAKUTAT* transferring survivors from the *FORT MERCER*. *Photos courtesy of U.S. Coast Guard, Boston, Mass.*

148

Drama on the high seas off Cape Cod when two oil tankers split in half at the same time. Another ship aground on Peaked Hill Bars in Provincetown.

Coast Guard Cutter *EASTWIND* and stern section of tanker *FORT MERCER* 30 miles southeast of Chatham after storm broke tanker in half. *Photo courtesy of U. S. Coast Guard.*

Nothing can compare with the violence surrounding a shipwreck at sea. Miles from the friendly· shore, tiny life boats, full of people, bob and heave atop giant waves that threaten to engulf them at any moment. When the sea abates, agonizing hours of waiting follow and only the strongest will live. Here the romance of the sea is forgotten and man is only interested in survival.

On February 18, 1952, a fierce northeast storm was lashing the coast. The Coast Guard men were busy helping out distressed fishing vessels along the shores when a call came into

Coast Guard personnel aboard the *YAKUTAT* working the rescue of a man on board the forward section of the *FORT MERCER*. This wreckage was later sunk with depth charges by the cutter *UNIMAK*. *Photo courtesy of U.S. Coast Guard, Boston, Mass.*

the Chatham station that the T-2 tanker *FORT MERCER* had sprung a leak 30 miles southeast of the station out in the Atlantic. Coast Guard units from Nantucket to Portland, Maine leaped into action and cutters were dispatched. The Salem Air station launched a PBY which flew out over the stricken ship. There were 60 foot seas and blinding snows to contend with, but the plane managed to stay with the wreck so that surface craft could zero in on the ship which had split into two pieces.

This was the kind of shipwreck drama on the high seas which makes widows and orphans. The two sections of the ship separated and the majority of the crew were on the stern section. One crewman was removed from the bow section by the Coast Guard. Later they had to sink the bow section with depth charges as it was a menace to navigation, floating around the ocean all alone. The stern section was towed to Block Island, Rhode Island by the tug *M. MORAN*.

The Coast Guard Cutter *EASTWIND* standing by the stern section of the *FORT MERCER*. The crew of the tanker waits on the fantail for pickup. *Photo courtesy of U.S. Coast Guard.*

Meanwhile, just a few miles off Cape Cod, another T-2 tanker was in the same type of trouble. The *PENDLETON*, overdue at Revere, was presumed to be riding out the storm. She too, had split in half after being hit by 60 foot waves, and the bow section was floating alone eight miles east of Chatham. The stern section of the *PENDLETON* floated by the *POLLOCK RIP LIGHTSHIP* and headed for Monomoy Island, south of Chatham with 33 men aboard. Aboard the stern section of the *PENDLETON*, the crewmen had been unable to radio the Coast Guard of their plight because all transmitting equipment was rendered inoperative when the ship split in two. It was ironic that the crew had a radio receiver still operating and were listening to news reports about the attempts to rescue the *FORT MERCER* and not a word about the *PENDLETON*.

The Coast Guard at Chatham however, knew all about the second ship as they had picked up the derelict hulk on their radar and were following the broken ship throughout the day. The amphibious DUKW was dispatched to go to the aid of the *PENDLETON*. but the small vehicle was unable to get close to the ship. A surfboat was sent out but mountainous seas sent them back without any success. With most of the heavy equipment of the Coast Guard concentrating on the rescue of the men of the *FORT MERCER* some thirty to fifty miles away, the responsibility of the men on board the *PENDLETON* fell to Boatswains Mate Bernard C. Webber of Eastham, stationed at Chatham. Webber manned a 36 foot motor lifeboat with three other crewmen; Richard P. Livesey, Irving Maske and Andrew Fitzgerald. These four men went out to the stern section of the *PENDLETON* and made an historic rescue which has gone down in the annals of the Coast Guard as one of the most dramatic and heroic rescues in the history of the service.

151

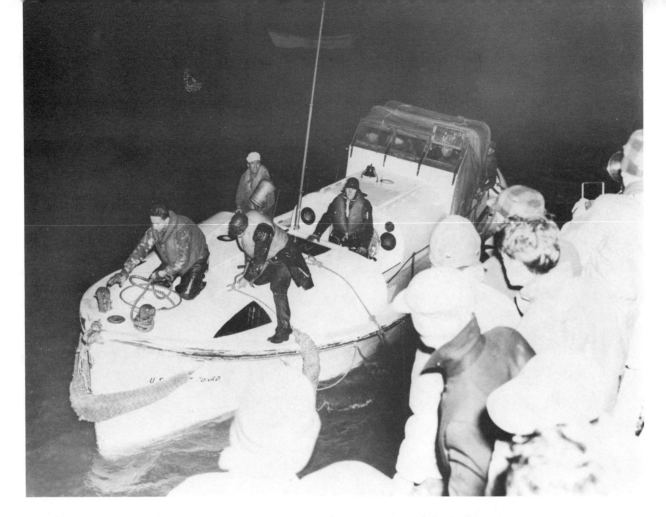

ABOVE: Survivors of *PENDLETON* wreck load into Coast Guard panel truck for the trip to the station after their ordeal at sea. OPPOSITE: TOP The Rescue Boat CG36500 returning to Chatham Fish Pier with 32 survivors of the tanker *PENDLETON* after their incredible rescue at sea. OPPOSITE BELOW: Coast Guardsman Bernie Webber (without hat) exhausted after battle with the ocean stands near the stern of the 36 foot motor lifeboat following return to Chatham. *Photos by Richard Cooper Kelsey, Chatham.*

Webber had a couple of strikes against him from the start, and without the Yankee cussedness of his type, might have failed the mission right away. As they were heading out over the bar, a giant wave hit the boat, smashed the windshield and carried away vital equipment for the task ahead. Most important, the boat's compass went overboard. Webber felt that to turn back at this point would be more dangerous than to continue, so they proceeded towards Pollock Rip, climbing over 20 to 30 foot seas on the way out.

Webber found the stern section of the *PENDLETON* and spotted the men aboard. They circled the vessel trying to determine the best course of action. With the ship rolling in the waves, rescue of the men seemed almost impossible in the conditions as they existed at the time. The *PENDLETON* had a port list. This, added to the rolling of the hull, made it possible for Webber to position his boat near the starboard side of the rolling ship, and the men aboard climbed down a Jacob's ladder and dropped the last few feet into the motor lifeboat.

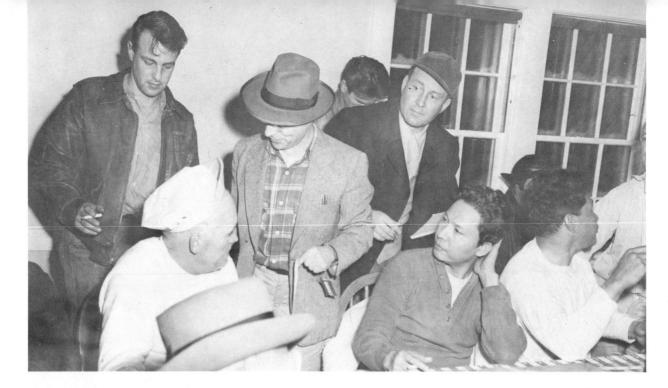

154

RIGHT: The Gold Lifesaving Medal. This rare award is a circular pendant, 1 and 7/16ths inches in diameter and 3/32nds of an inch in thickness and is 99.9 percent pure gold. This medal is awarded to those who risk their lives in order to save others from the perils of the sea. The Gold Lifesaving Medal is considered to be on a parallel with the Congressional Medal of Honor. The four crewmen of the Rescue Boat CG36500 were awarded this medal for their rescue of the 32 crewmen of the *PENDLETON*. *Photo by William P. Quinn.* OPPOSITE TOP: Benny Shufro of Puritan Clothing Company in Chatham with tape measure is taking measurements of the survivors of the *PENDLETON* for new clothes. OPPOSITE CENTER: The news media arrives. Two survivors of the *PENDLETON* wreck being interviewed for radio by Ed Semprini of WOCB in Yarmouth, Mass. OPPOSITE BELOW: The Gold Medal crew relax at the station following rescue of 32 crewmen of wrecked tanker *PENDLETON*. L to R Bernie Webber, Andrew J. Fitzgerald, Richard P. Livesey and Irving Maske. *Photos by Richard Cooper Kelsey, Chatham.*

There were 33 men aboard the *PENDLETON* and 32 men were successful in the transfer from the ship to the lifeboat. One man missed and was crushed between the lifeboat and the hull of the ship and was lost. With 36 souls aboard, Webber then turned the heavily laden surfboat toward the shore. He had no compass, but reversed his direction and put the waves behind him and headed in, figuring that he would hit the beach somewhere and he gave instructions for everyone to pile out quickly when the boat hit. Somehow, (Webber is convinced-the Almighty also had his hand on the wheel) the boat made it in over the Chatham Bar and Webber spotted the red light of the entrance buoy to Chatham Harbor. Just past that buoy was safety for all hands. The entire trip had been followed at the Chatham Coast Guard station on the Radar set, and when the boat pulled up to the dock at the Chatham Fish Pier, a large crowd had gathered to see the group come ashore and to congratulate the crew of the boat for a miraculous piece of rescue work.

The survivors were brought to the station in Chatham. There a good hot meal and warm clothing helped the morale of the rescued men. Reporters and photographers swarmed around the survivors of the *PENDLETON* and the crew of the motor lifeboat to record their story and tell the world what had happened. The next day, with calm seas, photographs were made of the bow and stern sections of the *PENDLETON*. The stern section still lays on the bar off Monomoy Island, a grim reminder of the past, rusting away with the sea eroding it, little by little. The derelict hull will remain for many more years before Mother Nature turns the metal into sea water.

TOP: The bow of the *PENDLETON* floating off Chatham. The photograph was taken Feb. 19, 1952, the day after the tanker broke in half in mountainous seas six miles off Chatham. *Photo by Richard Cooper Kelsey, Chatham.* ABOVE: This is the stern section of the tanker *PENDLETON* the morning after the wreck. Aerial photo taken by Richard Cooper Kelsey of Chatham shows the Jacobs ladder hanging over the side of the ship that the 32 men went down to the 36 foot motor lifeboat from Chatham the night before.

When the Coast Guard totalled up the day's events for the records, two tankers were split in two within 30 miles of each other off the Cape and 14 men lost their lives in the accidents. Seventy men were saved from the two vessels by the Coast Guard units involved. The *FORT MERCER's* stern was saved and reconstructed and renamed the *SAN JACINTO*. The fate of this vessel was not to be denied however, and on March 16, 1969, in a storm off the Virginia coast, the *SAN JACINTO* was ripped in half by a series of explosions 40 miles off shore. One man was killed in the mishap and the stern section was again towed into port.

No one knows what the mysterious magnetism is that draws a man to a life at sea. It is impossible to portray the trauma involved in a shipwreck such as this. Photographs of aftermath, taken the next day when the sky is clear and the sea is calm do not tell the story as vividly as the survivors described it. Sailors must be carved from the toughest sinew ever created, for when the excitement dies down, when the headlines read of other news, they return to the union halls, sign up on the next ship out, and once again turn their faces to the sea.

Close up view of *EVGENIA*, aground on Peaked Hill Bars 400 yards off shore, Provincetown, Mass. *Aerial photo by Quinn.*

Most of the shipwrecks on Cape Cod occur in the wintertime and the summer visitors miss seeing the drama. However, on September 8, 1953 the Panamanian registered freighter *EVGENIA* with all Greek crewmen ran aground on Peaked Hill Bars in Provincetown and was stuck there for all to see. It was right after Labor Day. There was still a good crowd staying on the Cape and there were many onlookers out in the storm when the Coast Guard set up the breeches buoy and started to bring the men ashore.

There were 24 crewmen aboard the *EVGENIA* at the time of the grounding and the ship held no cargo. She was on a run from St. John, N.B., to Baltimore, Maryland. Coast Guardsmen from Provincetown to Chatham took part in the rescue. They removed 12 men via the breeches buoy during the storm. The 13th man brought ashore in the buoy was unlucky, the hawser broke, dunking him in the surf close to shore and some of the summer tourists rushed into the water to pull him out. Four more men were brought ashore via the amphibious DUKW and seven men stayed aboard the ship to wait for a tugboat to pull them off.

The 255 foot freighter stayed on the bar for four days, and each day it worked closer into shore until finally, at low tide, visitors to the scene could reach out and touch the hull without getting their feet wet.

On September 12th, during a high course tide, the tug *CURB*, owned by Merritt-Chapman and Scott Corp., a N.Y. based salvage Co., hooked on to the 3,500 ton freighter and pulled her free of the Peaked Hill sands. The position of the ship had an effect on the final salvage. The ship was lying for the four days with her bow pointed towards the seas and therefore suffered no cracked plates or bad leaks. When she was pulled off, she could continue her trip without docking. But, while she was on Peaked Hill Bars, thousands of sightseers enjoyed their visit to the scene.

ABOVE: A Greek sailor rides the breeches buoy in over the raging surf to shore during the rescue of men from the *EVGENIA*. *Photo courtesy of Cape Cod National Seashore.* OPPOSITE: Panamanian freighter *EVGENIA*, 3500 tons from St. John, N. B. to Baltimore, Md. stuck on Peaked Hill Bars with lifeboat on shore. Lifeboat took some beating when it came through the waves at Peaked Hill. *Photo by John Bell, Provincetown.* BELOW: The *EVGENIA* laying near shore just prior to being towed off Peaked Hill Bars by the tug *CURB* of the Merrit, Chapman & Scott Salvage Company of N.Y. *Photo by John Bell, Provincetown.*

ABOVE: The *ALICE S. WENTWORTH*, for many years a familiar schooner in Cape Cod waters, was berthed in Woods Hole in 1962. *Photo by Wm. Quinn.* BELOW: Sunk at the dock. Many years of wear had taken their toll. She was raised, then sunk again. Raised again and beached. She was finally sold at auction to Lewis Athanas of Boston for use at the Pier 4 Restaurant only to break up at the dock during a storm. *Photo courtesy of the Cape Cod Standard Times, Hyannis, Mass.*

# CHAPTER 11

**"There's another wreck at the canal."**
**Shipwrecks occur in the waterway under all conditions**
**fair and foul and from sulphur to gypsum.**

MV *ARIZONA SWORD* sunk at the east end of the Cape Cod Canal after collision with *SS BERWINDVALE. Photo courtesy of Corps of Engineers.*

This chapter covers the last twenty plus years of incidents at the Cape Cod Canal. Groundings and collisions have occurred frequently during this period but in the future, automation may reduce these mishaps. Radar and closed circuit television, covering the entire 17 miles of the waterway give traffic dispatchers better control over vessels using the canal in both daytime and nighttime operations. The new equipment was installed in the early 1970's at the central control station near the railroad bridge at the west end of the canal. The accidents that have occurred in the canal over the past two decades had one positive note. There were no deaths or injuries to persons on the ships or to those assisting in the recovery of the people or property.

On May 5, 1951 the 3,133 ton *ARIZONA SWORD* with a cargo of 4,800 tons of bulk sulphur aboard was traveling east in the Cape Cod Canal. Shortly after clearing the Sagamore Bridge the vessel took a sheer to port. (1) During the same time, the 6,643 ton steam collier *BERWINDVALE* had just entered the east end of the canal and was traveling westerly in close proximity to the *ARIZONA SWORD*. Both vessels instituted actions to avoid collision but the *ARIZONA SWORD* was out of control and she continued her easterly motion broadside into the bow of the *BERWINDVALE*.

Salvage try on *ARIZONA SWORD*. pumps jet water out of the sunken hulk at the east end of the Cape Cod Canal. Salvage attempt took over one year to complete and remove cargo and ship. *Photo courtesy of Corps of Engineers.*

The collision occurred at 6:15 A.M. and the *ARIZONA SWORD* suffered a big hole in her starboard bow, five feet wide and seven feet deep and was taking on water. Day long efforts to control the flooding of the hull failed. The *ARIZONA SWORD* sank at 5 P.M. that afternoon on her port side at the east end of the canal hard by the north bank.

The ship sat in that position for a year before the cargo was taken off and the hull refloated. She was repaired and went back to sea. However, on January 13, 1961 the *ARIZONA SWORD* sank off Florida in a storm taking her crew of seven men to their deaths.

Note (1) When navigating in a narrow channel, a sheer is caused by bank cushion or bank suction. The ship continues its forward motion but the bow is pushed out into the center of the channel. Mariners can find regulations and recommendations covering sheers in chapter 12 of Knight's Seamanship. The accident with the Eastern Steamship Liner *BELFAST*, April 16, 1919 under the Sagamore Draw Bridge was caused by a sheer.

ABOVE: *ARIZONA SWORD* grounded at the east end of the Canal. The ship lay on the bottom for some months and gathered a good coat of barnacles before being pumped out and floated. BELOW: The starboard bow section of the *ARIZONA SWORD* with a gaping hole caused by collision with freighter *SS BERWINDVALE. SWORD* was salvaged and returned to service. *Photos courtesy of Corps of Engineers.*

ABOVE: A spectacular shipwreck in Buzzards Bay between two ships using the Cape Cod Canal. The Norwegian freighter *FERNVIEW* collided with the Sun Oil Company's *DYNAFUEL*. The *FERNVIEW'S* bow was imbedded 20 feet into the portside of the *DYNAFUEL*. Fire broke out immediately aboard the *DYNAFUEL* with smoke billowing 250 feet in the air. *Aerial photo by Quinn.* BELOW: During the height of the blaze the Coast Guard brought out all of the equipment they could muster to help fight the blaze and save the men. This photograph by Ronald Rolo of the New Bedford Standard Times has been used extensively by the Coast Guard on recruiting posters. *Photo courtesy of U.S. Coast Guard.*

After the fire had been put out, the big question was could they save the small vessel after they separated the two ships. This aerial photograph was taken about noon on Nov. 14th, 1963. *Aerial photo by Quinn.*

One of the more spectacular shipwrecks in the canal occurred on November 14, 1963 when the 6,732 ton Norwegian freighter *FERNVIEW* collided with the Sun Oil Company's 4,180 ton tanker *DYNAFUEL* at sunrise. The *FERNVIEW*'s bow was imbedded 20 feet into the portside of the *DYNAFUEL* after the collision. Crewmen of the tanker were taken aboard the freighter and then were evacuated by the Coast Guard.

The collision triggered the biggest Coast Guard rescue effort in years. Cutters, patrol planes, boats and helicopters were dispatched to the scene. A furious blaze was burning aboard the tanker and a massive effort was required to subdue the flames. A large black plume of smoke rose up from the wreck and was visible for miles.

When the two ships parted on the morning of the 15th the *DYNAFUEL* turned over and sank with her bow sticking up out of water. She stayed that way until salvagers towed her into New Bedford Harbor and cut her up for scrap. *Aerial photo by Quinn.*

At noontime, the Coast Guard had everything under control. The fire was out but the tanker was down ten feet in the water and in danger of sinking. That afternoon and evening the two vessels were held together while salvage experts surveyed the situation. Early in the morning, it was decided to separate the two ships. After the damaged vessels had been pulled apart, the *DYNAFUEL* slowly filled with water and then rolled over with its stern resting on the bottom in 35 feet of water in Buzzards Bay off Wings Neck. After a few months, the *DYNAFUEL* was towed into New Bedford upside down where the hull was cut up for scrap metal.

Salvage operations on the *SUSIE O. CARVER* at the east end of the Cape Cod
Canal off Scusset Beach. The *CARVER* was reported lost and divers found her in
52 feet of water. On Sept. 15, 1965, a dory and some wreckage drifted into the
Sandwich end of the Cape Cod Canal, the Captain of the fishing vessel has never
been found. *Photo by Gordon Caldwell, Hyannis.*

On November 23, 1965 the freighter *AMERICAN PILOT* rammed into the small tanker *MAUMEE SUN* in Buzzards Bay off Wings Neck near the entrance to the Cape Cod Canal. Tanker *SENIOR* unloading *MAUMEE SUN* cargo. *Photo by Gordon Caldwell, Hyannis.*

There was another ship collision in the canal very similar to the *FERNVIEW /  DYNAFUEL* clash in 1963. It was an ideal night, calm sea with perfect weather conditions. The 435 foot *AMERICAN PILOT* rammed into the little tanker *MAUMEE SUN* while she was carrying 483,000 gallons of fuel oil from Newark, New Jersey to Revere, Massachusetts.

The collision occurred on November 23, 1965 just a little over two years after the *FERNVIEW* and *DYNAFUEL*. This collision occurred also in Buzzards Bay near the Cleveland Ledge Lighthouse. There was no fire at the time and there were no injuries among the eleven crewmen aboard the *MAUMEE SUN*.

Soon after the collision it was discovered that the *MAUMEE SUN* was leaking oil badly. Officials of the oil company rushed another tanker to the scene to off load the cargo of the stricken vessel. Meanwhile the two ships had been lashed together so as to avoid losing the smaller vessel as had happened two years earlier.

Coast Guardsmen from the cutter *ACUSHNET* were aboard the *MAUMEE SUN* shoring up bulkheads for safety. After the cargo was off loaded, the two ships parted and with pumps aboard the *MAUMEE SUN*, she limped into port for repairs while the *AMERICAN PILOT* continued her journey.

ABOVE: Close up view of *AMERICAN PILOT* and *MAUMEE SUN* with the huge bow rammed into the smaller vessel in Buzzards Bay. Note cable connecting two vessels. BELOW: The *AMERICAN PILOT* maintained slight forward way to keep the two ships locked together so that the danger of the smaller vessel sinking could be avoided when the two ships parted. *Photos by Gordon Caldwell, Hyannis.*

ABOVE: The Coast Guard Cutter *YANKTON* cuts a path for a fishing boat through the ice in Buzzards Bay. Many smaller craft were trapped in the ice jam and had to be helped out during the 1968 January freeze. LEFT: 44 foot motor lifeboat in Hog Island channel inspecting an aid to navigation. The huge ice cakes made going tough even for the Coast Guard in spots, during January freeze. *Aerial photos by Gordon Caldwell, Hyannis.*

Right after New Years day in 1968, cold weather set in and continued for a few weeks. On January 15th the headlines in the papers outlined hardships caused by the sub-zero temperatures that were holding in for more than two weeks. At the Cape Cod Canal, a prolonged cold spell, with temperatures down below freezing for more than a week caused trouble for shipping.

During the second week in January the Coast Guard cutter *YANKTON*, a sea going tug, was kept busy making paths through the ice for New Bedford fishing boats while other Coast Guard craft were trying to keep the navigational aids on station so that ships that pass through the canal could do so without going aground.

The canal has fast currents that flow first east, then west as the tide changes. When floe ice is present, it can sometimes block the canal completely so that only the large ships can push through it. Some of these need a new boot top as the ice scrapes the paint off the hull as the ship passes through.

ABOVE: The Coast Guard buoy tender *HORNBEAM* picking up buoys in the Cape Cod Canal entrance in Buzzards Bay to keep them from being swept away by the ice. Ice buoys replaced the regular buoys during the cold weather period. *Aerial photo by Gordon Caldwell, Hyannis.* RIGHT: The regular buoys marking the western entrance to the Cape Cod Canal are piled up on State Pier in Buzzards Bay to wait out the cold spell. A stern reminder to ships passing to take care on the way down. *Photo by Quinn.*

Another problem is the buoys. The large ones have to be taken out so that the ice will not ruin them. They are piled up on State Pier at Buzzards Bay and ice spars are put out to serve during the cold spell. When these conditions exist, two buoy tenders from Woods Hole are busy around the clock to keep ahead of the ice. The potential for a ship going aground is highest at this period as navigation along the waterway without the regular buoys is extremely difficult.

Usually this condition lasts only a few days in the winter months and then things get back to normal. However in January of 1973 the freighter *GYPSUM QUEEN* went aground off Hog Island channel while the buoys were out because of expected ice. She freed herself on the next high tide. (See page 179.)

The Barge *FLORIDA* aground on the rocks near Silver Beach in Falmouth. The rocks made a big hole in the *FLORIDA* and 25,000 gallons of diesel fuel caused golden crested waves to break on Silver Beach. *Photo courtesy of the Falmouth Enterprise.*

In September of 1969, the barge *FLORIDA* while under tow in Buzzards Bay, broke loose from the tug and grounded on the rocks in Falmouth just south of Silver Beach with a stiff breeze blowing from the southwest. When the barge hit the rocks, holes were punched in the bottom and sides and 25,000 gallons of diesel fuel was let loose to foul the beaches and marine life for five miles either side of the wreck. Officials were on the scene and the clean up job began at once to try and save the marine life in the area.

Damage to the beaches was cleaned up quickly but the oil did not float entirely and much of it sank to the bottom and the marine life kill was uncountable. The areas in West Falmouth were closed for all types of shellfishing and four years later in 1973 many are still closed.

Dr. Max Blumer of the Woods Hole Oceanographic Institution carried out an extensive study of the oil spill throughout the area and found that the contamination was widespread. Lobsters, clams, crabs and many other types of marine life washed ashore on the beaches for weeks after the spill occurred. The oil is ingested by the animals and the hydrocarbons remain in the tissues and cannot be flushed out by the natural process. The entire food chain of marine life is affected by the petroleum in the water. Hydrocarbons in shellfish if eaten by humans can cause cancer so the clam flats are still closed.

Officials are still not certain as to the length of time it will take before the area is safe again and in the meantime the oil company had to pay the town of Falmouth $100,000 in damages for the oil spill.

ABOVE: One of life's embarrassing moments. The sloop *BETTY D* with six persons aboard grounded at the east end of the Cape Cod Canal early in the morning of May 29, 1968. The call to the Coast Guard for aid in this precarious spot piled up two Coast Guard boats while the people aboard the sloop were led to safety over the granite jetty. All of the grounded boats were lifted off gently the next day by a crane.
BELOW: A good crowd gathered at noon on Sunday, Feb. 1, 1970 when the 444 foot Italian freighter *PAOLA COSTA* ran aground just west of the Sagamore Bridge in the Cape Cod Canal. The steering mechanism had gone out of control and the anchor was dropped just as the vessel hit the granite riprap on the north side of the canal. *Photos by Quinn.*

On February 1, 1970 the Italian freighter *PAOLA COSTA* hit the granite rip-rap on the north side of the Cape Cod Canal just west of the Sagamore Bridge. The cause of the accident was listed as a faulty steering mechanism. The freighter dropped anchor just after hitting the rip-rap. There was a stiff eastward current running and the men aboard the freighter had to have some degree of control or the current would have carried the ship back into the supports of the Sagamore Bridge.

173

ABOVE: The tug *MANAMET* put a line aboard the *PAOLA COSTA* and pulled her free of the strong easterly tide run and out into the center of the Canal so that she could proceed without further damage. BELOW: After nearing the center of the Canal the *PAOLA COSTA* was able to proceed under her own power. Later inspection at the west end of the Canal showed that the ship suffered no damage from the temporary grounding. *Photos by Quinn.*

The ship was on the north side of the canal and with the fast moving current, could not work her way off the rocks. Within an hour, the tug *MANAMET* from the Army Corps of Engineers in Buzzards Bay was alongside the freighter and put a line aboard and pulled the vessel back into the center of the canal where she was able to proceed to the west end for inspection. Repairs to the steering mechanism had been made and the freighter continued its voyage to New York.

The *PAOLA COSTA* was 6,594 tons enroute from Boston, Mass. to New York City with 3,047 tons of general cargo.

RIGHT: Early on the morning of March 16, 1971 the Allied Chemical Oil *BARGE #11* was grounded near #8 buoy in Hog Island channel at the west entrance to the Cape Cod Canal. The barge carried 1800 tons of Tar oil. High winds carried the barge into shoal water during a change in tie-up with her tug. *Aerial photo by Quinn.* ABOVE: The barge was hard aground and had to be unloaded to free her from the mud. A couple of days later while the barge was being unloaded a New Bedford fishing dragger the *ELLEN & MARIE* went around the barge on the wrong side and became hard aground herself for a few hours. *Photo by Quinn.*

Early on the morning of March 16, 1971 the Allied Chemical Oil *BARGE # 11* was grounded near #8 buoy in Hog Island channel at the west entrance to the canal. The barge was being towed by the tug *J. H. DEINLEIN* and was bound from Philadelphia to Bangor, Maine. The barge was loaded with 1,800 tons of tar oil. The official reports to the Coast Guard relate that high winds carried the barge onto the shoal water during a change in tie-up with the tug.

The barge was drawing 13′-6″ of water and she was aground in 13′ of water. During the next high tide the following morning the tug *DEINLEIN* was joined by the Corps of Engineers tug *MANAMET* and the two tugs tried without success to pull the barge free. The barge was out of the regular channel so canal traffic was not affected by the grounding.

The next morning, a New Bedford fishing boat, the *ELLEN & MARIE* was clearing the canal and decided to go around the barge on the wrong side and ran aground herself and stayed stuck for a few hours until the Coast Guard could pull her off the shoals. Soon another barge arrived at the scene and the cargo was pumped out of *BARGE #11* and she began to float. They pumped her cargo back into her and she left for Maine. There was no oil spill during the grounding or the transfers of cargo back and forth but with the barge sitting so close to the heavily traveled channel, the potential for a collision by another vessel in fog or storm was very real in the eyes of the crews.

During the entire two days that the barge was aground, the Coast Guard had a vessel on duty at the scene around the clock just in case of an oil spill. Efforts could be started at once to correct the situation before much damage could be done.

ABOVE: The United States Navy Destroyer *HARLAN R. DICKSON* had a power failure and was aground on the stone jetty at the east end of the Cape Cod Canal for 10½ hours on July 27, 1971. This was during the summer season and the destroyer attracted thousands of tourists to the end of the canal. BELOW: After the tide dropped, the *DICKSON* started to heel over and show her bottom. The destroyer was freed at 3 A.M. the next morning with the help of the Corps of Engineers tug *MANAMET* and some natural aid in the form of an 8 foot tide. *Photos by Quinn.*

On July 27, 1971 a mysterious power failure caused the Navy destroyer *HARLAN R. DICKSON* to veer out of the channel and ground near the rock jetty at the east end of the Cape Cod Canal.

The destroyer was underway with a pilot aboard entering the canal under normal conditions when the power failure occurred. Rudolph Gendron, veteran canal pilot, was in control of the ship at the time. "All power suddenly went out. It was the oddest sensation I have ever experienced. I was able to get off one blast of the whistle to warn small boats in the area and heel the wheel hard to port." "The circuits were tried" Gendron said, "about 20 minutes after the ship settled in soft sand just inches from the sandcatcher (underwater jetty) and everything worked, but the tide was on the ebb and she was fast aground."

More than 200 bathers, fishermen and boat watchers, who had gathered near the canal entrance to watch the destroyer go through, were amazed when she suddenly turned and headed for the beach after sounding one blast from her whistle. The grounding occurred right in the middle of summer, so there was no shortage of sightseers in the area.

With the destroyer parked in the sand, right at the end of the jetty, it appeared to be aground on the rocks. Many people walked out on the jetty at low tide to get close to the ship and to talk with the sailors on board.

At 3 A.M. the next morning, the tug *MANAMET* pulled the *HARLAN R. DICKSON* free on an eight foot tide. Naval divers were sent down to inspect the hull and they found no damage. At five A.M. the destroyer left for Boston to go into the Navy Yard to determine the cause of the accident at the canal.

The 97 foot New Bedford fishing dragger *SAO PEDRO* tipped up on the breakwater at the east end of the Cape Cod Canal on July 14, 1972. Another embarrassing moment with a radar perched atop the pilot house of the boat and coming to grief at a radar reflector on the end of the breakwater is almost unexplainable. *Photo by Quinn.*

On July 14, 1972 the 97 foot New Bedford dragger *SAO PEDRO* with a crew of six aboard climbed the breakwater on the north side of the east end entrance to the Cape Cod Canal. The vessel had on board 12,000 pounds of fish. She apparently missed the entrance and became lodged on the granite breakwater right in front of the radar reflecting beacon and fog horn.

The location of the wreck was less than one mile from the Sandwich Coast Guard station. The vessel came ashore at 3 A.M. and for twelve hours sat in a precarious position in danger of sinking right at the entrance to the canal. The damage to the hull was limited to the forward keel section which was badly battered by the impact when the boat hit the granite. This damage was fully visible as the tide dropped throughout the morning.                177

The *SAO PEDRO* waiting for the tide to come up to get free from the rocks. No one was injured in the mishap but the forward keel section was badly broken by the impact of colliding with the breakwater. The boat was freed in the afternoon at high tide. *Photo by Quinn.*

The boat was perched on the end of the breakwater and caused many chuckles among the many summer visitors to Cape Cod who strolled down to the end of the breakwater to get a close look at the boat. The event however, was no treat for the owners and crewmen of the vessel. The man at the wheel had completely missed his bearings when he entered the canal and the boat fetched up on the rocks.

About 2 P.M. that afternoon the Army Corps of Engineers tug *MANAMET* gave a gentle pull and the *SAO PEDRO* slid off the rocks and into deep water. Not only had a large crowd gathered on shore to watch the operations but a large number of pleasure craft were parked all around the end of the canal to watch the salvage efforts.

The 436' *GYPSUM QUEEN* aground at Stoney Point dike. The ship freed herself at high tide seven hours later. She was loaded with 10, 294 tons of plaster. *Photo by Gordon Caldwell, Hyannis, Mass.*

The *GYPSUM QUEEN* was a case of another grounding in Hog Island channel at the west end of the canal. It was late on the morning of January 19, 1973 and the regular buoys at the west end of the canal had been removed due to expected ice.

The *GYPSUM QUEEN* was clearing the canal and heading for Philadelphia with 10,294 tons of gypsum when she had to veer out of the channel to avoid a collision with an oncoming freighter.

The ship lay on the shoal through one tide and freed herself on the next high tide. She was out of Hantsport, Nova Scotia with a crew of 28 men and there were no injuries and no damage to the ship's hull.

TOP: At 10:30 A.M. on October 14, 1973 the 445 foot *ARIZPA* out of Wilmington, Delaware, bound for Boston, Mass. went aground at the east end of the Cape Cod Canal. Traffic in the canal was halted for three hours until she was floated free on the high tide. ABOVE: The modern method of shipping is by containerized cargo. The *ARIZPA* carried 3,700 tons of this cargo and was aided by the Corps of Engineers tug *MANAMET* from Buzzards Bay. BELOW: The cargo containers piled high on deck acted as a sail and stiff northwest winds pushed the ship aground. After refloating, the vessel continued on to Boston. *Photos by Quinn.*

# CHAPTER 12

**Collision at Sea . . . The memorable disaster of the**
*ANDREA DORIA* **and the** *STOCKHOLM* **in 1956.**
**The** *HORNBEAM* **in 1972.**

*I'M ALONE.* Chatham fishing boat aground on Monomoy Point south of Chatham, April, 1956. Boat suffered damage and was beyond salvage. She had to be abandoned. *Aerial photo by Quinn.*

In 1956 a small fishing boat was wrecked on Cape Cod. In April the Chatham fisherman *I'M ALONE* was at Butler Hole, off Monomoy, fishing at night. When the boat left the fishing ground to return to port they missed a buoy and ran aground on Monomoy Point.

The boat was caught in the surf and the crew was unable to get it off the sand. The vessel suffered further damage in a storm following the grounding and was a total loss.

Just as many old time schooner Captains had their fortunes invested in their ships, the modern fishing Captain on the Cape has a good share of equity in his fishing boat. The *I'M ALONE* loss was measured in the thousands in direct contrast with the next wreck in 1956 which was measured in the millions.

Aerial photo of *ANDREA DORIA* taken about 8 A.M. on the morning after the collision with the *STOCKHOLM* 50 miles south of Nantucket. *Photo courtesy of U. S. Coast Guard.*

Many will call it the shipwreck of the century. The proportionately small number of deaths may reduce the importance of the event. However, the drama involved includes a thousand different stories pertaining to the personal incidents in the tragedy.

It was late in the evening of July 25, 1956 and the Queen of the Italian line, *ANDREA DORIA*, was steaming towards New York City, fifty miles south of Nantucket Island. The crew and passengers were making plans for the following morning when they would arrive in the city. The Swedish motor vessel *STOCKHOLM* had left New York that day and was sailing east. There were fog banks on the ocean that night. Ships would sail in and out of the fog so that radar was of a prime necessity.

Just how it happened, or why, is still being argued, but the *STOCKHOLM*, with an extra strong bow for plowing through ice-filled northern European waters, sliced into the side of the three year old pride of the Italian fleet. The *STOCKHOLM'S* bow knifed a third of the way through the forward section of the *ANDREA DORIA* near the bridge and, unfortunately, hit the empty fuel tanks in the lower decks of the *DORIA*, filling them with sea water and causing the liner to take an immediate starboard list.

ABOVE: The eight lifeboats on the port side could not be lowered because of the immediate list the ship took after being hit by the *STOCK-HOLM*. This photo was made at approximately 9 A.M. on the morning of July 26, 1956. Most of the passengers and crew were off the *ANDREA DORIA* at this time. BELOW: The *STOCKHOLM*. At the bow, the damage is monumental while at the stern, injured are being flown to hospitals by U.S. Air Force helicopters from Otis A.F.B., Cape Cod and by U.S. Coast Guard helicopters from Salem Air Station. *Photos by U.S. Coast Guard.*

It was 11:09 P.M. By midnight radios were broadcasting the messages throughout the New England area. Every ship within 100 miles of the accident raced to the scene. In one of history's greatest rescue operations at sea, when the other ships took on most of the 1,709 passengers from the stricken liner.

Fifty-two died, either aboard the crippled ship, during the collision or in the fog shrouded waters. For eleven hours, while rescue operations were underway, the Italian liner stayed afloat. Then at 10:09 A.M. the following day the *ANDREA DORIA*, abandoned by all but the dead on board, turned over and sank in 225 feet of water where she rests today.

Much time and effort has been spent trying to figure a way to bring up the sunken liner. Most of the ideas are pipe dreams and need better technology before they can be implemented. There was reported to be a million dollars in cash, and over three million more in other valuables that went down with the ship. The fortune may never be recovered. The hull lies in over 250 feet of water and at that depth, divers can only work for short periods of time and then not efficiently.

Using an underwater habitat, divers went down to the *ANDREA DORIA* in the summer of 1973. The group engaged in the salvage reported that they were unsuccessful in recovering any of the treasure aboard the sunken liner.

It is ironic, however, that this should ever have happened. And, but for international laws governing the sea, the *ANDREA DORIA* might still be sailing today. When the Coast Guard cutter *HORNBEAM* arrived on the scene, early in the morning, she wanted to take the ship in tow to shallow waters, so that if she sank she would rest on the bottom with most of the hull above water. Salvage, in that position, would have been relatively easy and only a matter of days. There was a shoal nearby where the water was only 70 feet deep. Without a release for the responsibility of the ship (she was foreign registry) the *HORNBEAM* could not put a line aboard the stricken vessel. About 9:30 A.M., the word came through granting permission for the tow but by then it was too late. The main deck was under water and it was the beginning of the end of the *ANDREA DORIA*. The Captain and the last remaining crewmen came aboard the *HORNBEAM* and were brought ashore, sad, but alive.

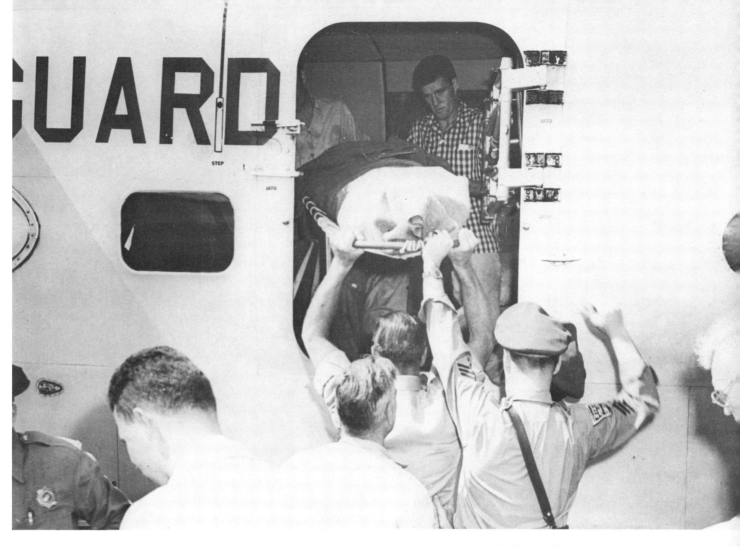

OPPOSITE ABOVE: The U. S. Coast Guard cutter *HORNBEAM*, a buoy tender out of Woods Hole, Mass. is on the scene and is shown receiving the crew of the *ANDREA DORIA* from her lifeboats, the stricken ship is in the background left. ABOVE: A survivor is unloaded from a Coast Guard amphibious plane at Logan Airport in Boston, Mass. State Police and volunteers aid in speeding injured to hospitals. RIGHT: Survivors of the *ANDREA DORIA/STOCKHOLM* collision were flown to hospitals in Boston by the Coast Guard as soon as the helicopters touched down at Nantucket with the injured. *Photos by U. S. Coast Guard.*

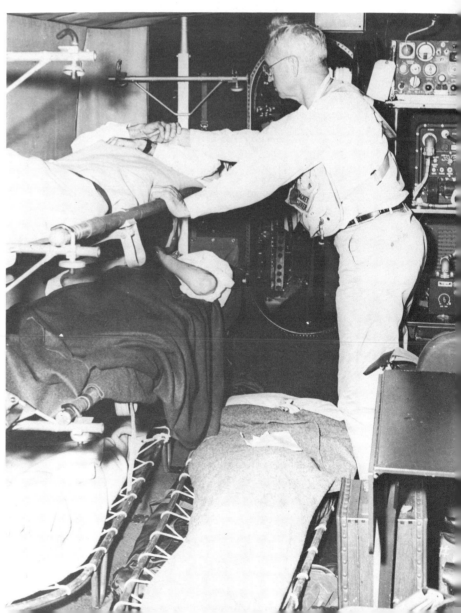

The *ANDREA DORIA* turns
over and takes her final plunge
to the bottom of the ocean. This is a
Pulitzer Prize winning photograph taken
by Harry Trask, copyright - Boston Herald Traveler.

A close-up shot of the huge gash in the bow of the Coast Guard Cutter *HORNBEAM*, rammed by a Brazilian freighter 40 miles southwest of Nantucket. The *HORNBEAM* was on her way to service the *NANTUCKET LIGHTSHIP* when she was rammed by the *DOCELAGO*. *Aerial photo by Quinn.*

Sometimes the dull monotonous duty aboard the Coast Guard buoy tenders can be jolted into a little excitement. A case in point happened late on a Wednesday night, May 24, 1972, when the 555 foot Brazilian freighter *DOCELAGO* slashed into the forward starboard side of the 180 foot buoy tender *HORNBEAM*, 40 miles southwest of Nantucket Island.

The crash left a huge wedge shaped hole on the forward section of the *HORNBEAM*, but most of the damage was above the water line. The forward hold of the ship was flooded but pumps were able to keep the vessel afloat.

There were no injuries among the crew of 45 officers and men on board the *HORNBEAM*. The freighter suffered little damage and she stayed by the buoy tender until two other Coast Guard cutters arrived at the scene to escort her back into port.

The *HORNBEAM* arrived back at State Pier in Buzzards Bay fifteen hours later and stopped for officials to inspect the damage. The cutter went to the Boston Navy yard for repairs. She was back in service again within a few months.

The *HORNBEAM* is stationed in Woods Hole. Her primary duty is the maintainence of navigational aids in waters of the First Coast Guard District. The *HORNBEAM* was one of the first ships on the scene to aid the stricken liner *ANDREA DORIA* in 1956, when that vessel was in collision with the Swedish Motor Vessel *STOCKHOLM*. Ironically, the *HORNBEAM* was rammed herself near the spot in the Atlantic where the *ANDREA DORIA* was hit, 40 miles south of Nantucket Island.

The Coast Guard Cutter *HORNBEAM* collided with the 555 foot Brazilian freighter *DOCELAGO* 40 miles southwest of Nantucket at 11 P.M. May 24, 1972. The *HORNBEAM* suffered a large gash in her bow and was limping back to port the next day when the photo was taken. *Aerial photo by Quinn.*

# CHAPTER 13

Today's Coast Guard. Radar and computerized jet helicopters
have replaced the Life Saver on beach patrol with his
rubber boots and kerosene lanterns.

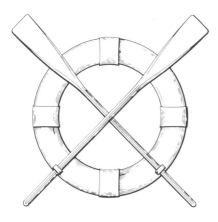

LEFT: Early Surfman's insignia of the
United States Coast Guard. RIGHT: The
crossed anchors and shield, official insignia of today's Coast Guard.

On July 25, 1972 a storm was kicking up along the coast and at 4:20 P.M., a 40 foot
utility boat was called away from Coast Guard base, Woods Hole, to go to the aid of the
*NOAH A,* a 56 foot dragger, aground near New Bedford.

The boat was piloted by BM-2 John J. LaBrier. Others on the boat were seaman Richard
Damon and engineer Michael Gorin. The Coast Guard boat proceeded to the scene and stood
by with pumps as a commercial tug pulled the dragger free. While at this job, the boat received a radio call to proceed to the aid of a second fishing dragger with engine failure,
anchored in Buzzards Bay. The Coast Guardsmen located the 88 foot *SILVER BAY* and
towed her into New Bedford. While towing the dragger in, the Coast Guard boat lost all of
her electronic aids. Radar, fathometer, lights and the two way radio was only receiving
messages from the base. The transmitter was inoperative. The 40 footer left New Bedford
at 9 P.M. and headed back to her base at Woods Hole.

The boat was entering Woods Hole passage and the crew spotted a lobster boat aground
on Weepecket Island signaling for help. They pulled the lobsterman free and towed him into
Hadley's Harbor. A little after 10 P.M. the crew of the Coast Guard boat returned to their
base with only their engine working. They tied up the boat and walked into the mess hall,
grabbed a couple of sandwiches and then jumped aboard another 40 foot boat, (this one an
open boat with no cabin for protection) and went back out on another rescue call.

The latest call took them into the waters of Vineyard Sound and Buzzards Bay searching
for two overdue small craft; an 18 foot sailboat with two people on board and a 12 foot
sailboat with one youngster aboard. The search continued and while on this duty the crew
of the 40 foot boat was diverted to aid a 26 foot sailboat that had stranded on the rocks at
Quisset Harbor. They removed three people and their belongings from the stranded sailboat
and set cradle bumpers around the craft to prevent tide damage. The Coast Guardsmen were
aided in this rescue by a civilian in a small Boston Whaler.

After this the crew resumed the search for the other two lost sailboats. They stayed on
this duty until both boats had been found and then returned to the base at Woods Hole at
6:30 A.M. on July 26th, tied up their boat and finished a fourteen hour rescue call. Other
units of the Coast Guard were on duty that night as well. A 44 foot motor lifeboat and the
82 foot *POINT TURNER* had also been engaged in the rescue of four other vessels and a
reported plane crash, in addition to the search for the two lost sailboats.

Revenue Cutter Massachusetts

Richard Plean

The first cutter. The *MASSACHUSETTS*. The ship was built and launched at Newburyport, Massachusetts in 1791. Fifty feet long with a 17 foot 8 inch beam she was 70.5 tons. The cutter was armed with six swivel guns. The *MASSACHUSETTS* was the largest of the "ten boats" ordered by Alexander Hamiliton to institute the United States Revenue Cutter Service. *Reproduction courtesy U.S.C.G., Boston, Mass.*

In 1790, Alexander Hamilton asked Congress for ten boats to form the Revenue Marine Service. This was the birth of today's Coast Guard. The ten cutters were the 70 ton *MASSA-CHUSETTS*, the 51 ton *SCAMMEL*, the 50 ton vessels *ACTIVE* and *PICKERING*, the 40 ton *DILLIGENCE*, the 35 ton vessels *ARGUS*, *VIGILANT*, *VIRGINIA* and *SOUTH CAROLINA* and the 30 ton *GENERAL GREENE*. They began a service to this country that is spread all over the world today. The varied duty of the modern Coast Guard covers a wide range, from saving life and property at sea, to a separate military force called on in time of war to protect the country against its enemies.

Today's Life Saver is a hundred giant steps from his predecessor who tramped the beaches for endless miles searching for shipwrecks and the survivors. The rubber boots and coston signals have been replaced with the most modern system of life saving that man can assemble with up to date technology and jet age speed. Had the Monomoy Disaster event (1902, Pg. 63) occurred today, a radio call on the emergency frequency of the Coast Guard would bring a twin turbine jet helicopter to the scene in minutes and the five men would have been picked off the grounded barge without even getting their feet wet.

After formation in 1915 from the Revenue Cutter Service and the Life Saving Service the Coast Guard carried on the traditions set forth in the early days and from 1915 to 1940 the advances in technology improved the service to the point where with the coming of World War II the Coast Guard went into action with the U. S. Navy. The men of the Coast Guard were called on to assume additional duties in the global conflict. They convoyed cargo ships across the Atlantic and screened troop transports. However, the most vital service performed was the anti-submarine warfare, waged against the Germans in the Atlantic and the Japanese in the Pacific. The ships and aircraft of the Coast Guard took a heavy toll of the German U-boats.

ABOVE: The high endurance cutter *HAMILTON*, 378 feet, stationed at Boston, Mass. The cutter was named after the man who created the Revenue Cutter Service in 1790. She is the largest ever built for Coast Guard duty and is the most modern in 1973. BELOW: A Cape Cod HH-52A helicopter, dubbed the "Flying Lifeboat", sets down atop the 210 foot *DECISIVE*, a medium endurance cutter. The 70 foot flight deck gives pilots room to set down easily for transfer of personnel and material at sea. *Photos courtesy of U.S. Coast Guard.*

ABOVE: The 95 foot *CAPE CROSS*. Her 2,300 horsepower drives her over the waves at 20 knots. A fast patrol boat for inshore work. BELOW: The 82 foot *POINT HANNON*. The small patrol boats are used for a variety of duties from law enforcement to search and rescue. *Photos courtesy of U.S. Coast Guard.*

ABOVE: U.S. Coast Guard icebreaker *STATEN ISLAND* is a veteran of icebreaking missions in the Arctic as well as the Antarctic Operation Deep Freeze support missions for U. S. scientific programs. Built in 1943, she was formerly the Navy *AGB-5* until transferred to the Coast Guard February 1, 1966. *Photo courtesy of U.S. Coast Guard.*

ABOVE: 40 and 44 foot motor lifeboats are the utility craft for the Coast Guard. The 40 foot boat is used on most inland water search and rescue while the 44 foot self-bailing, self-righting motor lifeboat is among the most versatile of all of the small boats of the service. BELOW: The newest addition to the Coast Guard fleet is the 41 foot motor lifeboat. Built for speed and durability, the boat has an aluminum hull with a fiberglass superstructure. It is equipped with twin 275 H.P. diesel engines that drive it at a top speed of 24 knots with a range of 300 miles. The boat carries a crew of 3 and has a capacity of 21 passengers. *Photos by U.S. Coast Guard, Boston, Mass.*

193

The pleasure schooner went to war in the 1940's. Coast Guard Reserves manned wooden yachts and carried out submarine patrols from the coast of Massachusetts down to New York. *Photo courtesy U.S. Coast Guard, Boston, Mass.*

A little known but epic arm of the Coast Guard in the submarine war was the Corsair Fleet of World War II. These men went to sea in silent sailing craft, two masted sloops and yachts armed with only small machine guns and raw courage. They ranged from the Massachusetts Coast down to New York. Their base of operations was at the Boston Naval Annex.

About two dozen wooden hulled craft, former yachts and fishing boats, manned by the Coast Guard Reservists went out in all kinds of weather and stalked the U-boats in the shipping lanes near the coast. Under full sail the Corsairs carried on their mission under the guise of a pleasure cruise. When they spotted a submarine, they would keep it in sight if it stayed near the surface and if not, the boats were equipped with hydrophones to track the sub underwater. A radio call to the combat units nearby and on shore would bring planes and surface craft to the scene to drop depth charges on the sub while the yacht would move to a safer position and watch the action.

The Corsair had no armament and was a sitting duck should a U-boat come to the surface and engage the deck gun. A couple of shells could blow the yacht to pieces and kill all on board. However, their stealth and uncanny luck enabled them to go undiscovered by the submarine commanders and none of the World War II sailing vessels were ever lost.

The schooner under full sail was the silent listening post off-shore. The most picturesque members of the fleet of Coast Guard Reserves in World War II. *Photo courtesy of U.S.C.G., Boston, Mass.*

On watch, ever alert. The beautiful but slow sailing vessels took their toll of Nazi U-boats during World War II. *Photo courtesy U.S.C.G., Boston, Mass.*

The majority of the Corsair Fleet were built for summer pleasure cruises. These boats were not equipped with heating systems. The Coast Guard Reserves improvised somewhat and constructed deck houses around the wheel and binnacle area to afford protection against the cold weather for the man at the helm. The men on deck had to bundle up for warmth with heavy waterproof clothing. Despite these precautions, the chill factor on the North Atlantic with the wind blowing 30 or 40 MPH and the temperature down around 20 degrees must have been extremely piercing. The men on the picturesque schooners carried out hazardous duty in the time honored traditions of iron men and wooden ships.

ABOVE: The *WHITE SAGE*, buoy tender based at Woods Hole, Mass. *Photo courtesy of U.S. Coast Guard.*

There are myriad duties carried out by the Coast Guard today. The modern cutters hold duty weather stations in both the Atlantic and Pacific oceans, participate in the International Ice Patrol keeping an eye on icebergs near the shipping lanes and in the polar regions the Coast Guard ice breakers open passages for domestic use. They are charged with enforcing our federal laws on the high seas and patroling the foreign fishing fleet on the continental shelf to insure against violation of the international fishing treaties.

The Coast Guard maintains a complex set of aids to navigation on all of the country's waterways and sea coasts. Thousands of buoys are set, replaced and serviced each year in the harbors and shipping lanes on the east and west coasts and the Great Lakes. The picturesque lighthouses that complement our shorelines are manned or automated by the Coast Guard which took over from the civilian lighthouse service in 1939.

ABOVE: Nauset Lighthouse in Eastham is automated and requires no keeper so the house was sold to private ownership. BELOW: The Nobska Point Lighthouse looks out over Vineyard Sound in Woods Hole. *Photos by Quinn.*

ABOVE: Highland Lighthouse in Truro is one of the Cape's most famous landmarks. *Photo by Quinn.* BELOW: Wood End Lighthouse in Provincetown, Mass. *Photo courtesy of U.S. Coast Guard, Boston.*

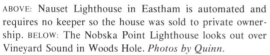

**COAST GUARD**
LIGHT STATION NOBSKA POINT

The *NANTUCKET LIGHTSHIP* underway to her station, fifty miles southeast of Nantucket Island at the end of the Nantucket Shoals. The ship stands on her station year round. *Photo courtesy U.S. Coast Guard, Boston, Mass.*

Lightships were considered tedious duty but have almost all been replaced by towers and buoys. However, some like the *NANTUCKET SHOALS LIGHTSHIP*, 60 miles southeast of Nantucket Island, are too far out at sea to be replaced and will continue on duty station until modern technology solves the replacement problem. Long range aids to navigation (LORAN) stations are manned by Coast Guard personnel in all parts of the world.

The Coast Guard enforces the federal laws pertaining to the Merchant Marine. American vessels are inspected by officials of the Coast Guard in order to insure all safety regulations for passengers and crew are adhered to by owners. Also included are periodic inspections of hulls, machinery and equipment of all vessels for seaworthiness and examination of all crewmen engaged in the supervision of the running of the ships.

198

ABOVE LEFT: Buzzards Bay Light Tower. These towers are replacing lightships all along the coasts of the U.S. where a buoy will not serve as a navigational aid. This tower is located four miles west of Cuttyhunk Island in Buzzards Bay and is manned by the Coast Guard. *Photo courtesy of U.S. Coast Guard, Boston, Mass.* ABOVE RIGHT: The *STONEHORSE LIGHTSHIP* was stationed about a mile off the southeast tip of Monomoy Point. She was replaced by a fixed tower on Oct. 15, 1963. BELOW: The *POLLOCK RIP LIGHTSHIP* was stationed six miles southeast of Chatham Lighthouse. She was replaced by a buoy on July 1, 1969. *Photos by Quinn.*

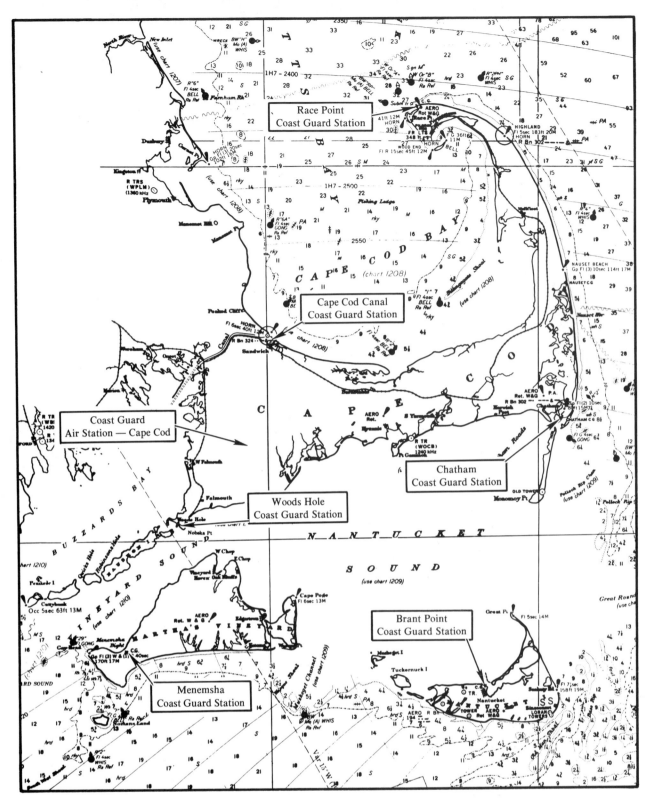

The seven Coast Guard installations covering Cape Cod and the Islands. *Reproduction from Chart #1107.*

The lifeboat stations are still an integral part of the Coast Guard today and these too have been modernized. On the backside of Cape Cod two of the original thirteen are still manned today. The improvements in rescue techniques, 2-way radio communications and radar have made beach patrols obsolete and amphibious vehicles have retired the hand rowed lifeboat and the kerosene lanterns so that two stations can do the work that once required thirteen. Race Point in Provincetown and the Chatham station maintain a constant readiness for trouble on the backside. The Woods Hole complex supports a lifeboat station and a buoy maintainence shop. The Cape Cod Canal station in Sandwich serves the Canal and Cape Cod Bay areas. On Nantucket the Brant Point station and on Martha's Vineyard the Menemsha station service the off shore islands.

ABOVE: Aerial photograph of the Woods Hole Station with the buoy repair shops. Coast Guard cutters and patrol boats at the pier. At the upper center of the picture are the ferries to Martha's Vineyard and Nantucket. To the upper right is the Woods Hole Scientific community. RIGHT: The Race Point Station in Provincetown at the northern tip of Cape Cod. BELOW LEFT: Chatham Lighthouse, Chatham Coast Guard Station and the LARC-V going out on a rescue call. The amphibious vehicle was named from her long title — Lighter Amphibious Reconnaissance Craft. An aluminum hull vehicle. BELOW RIGHT: The Cape Cod Canal Station in Sandwich situated at the east end of the Canal. *Photos by Quinn.*

ABOVE: 70 miles northeast of Provincetown, Monday afternoon Jan. 24, 1966 with rudder and power gone, the 455 foot freighter *SOUTH AFRICAN VICTORY*, listing 30 degrees, lay dead in the water, battered by 40-foot seas and 50 knot winds. A Coast Guard plane circled overhead as a helicopter and the cutters *ACUSHNET*, *BIBB*, and *CACTUS* rushed to the scene. Later the freighter regained power and rudder and was able to limp into port with her three cutter escort. The photo shows the ship making headway under reduced power and with a severe list to port. She moored at Boston Army Base at 7 P.M. on Jan. 25, 1966. None of her crew of 48 or her five passengers were injured. OPPOSITE ABOVE: The Coast Guard to the rescue — covering a multitude of troubles aboard the *CARA CARA* in Massachusetts Bay off Scituate on Sept. 13, 1966. Five Coast Guard units at the scene. The helicopter is dropping a basket to bring up a injured man to transfer him to a hospital. OPPOSITE BELOW: The Gloucester fisherman *JACKIE B* afire offshore with a Coast Guard boat alongside with firefighting equipment in action. *Photos courtesy of U.S. Coast Guard, Boston, Mass.*

Their motto is "Semper Paratus", always ready. Officers and men of the Coast Guard have to be ever alert. There are times when the many duties will manifest themselves on top of each other. Sometimes a routine patrol will turn into a rescue mission or involve law enforcement. In the summertime the Coast Guard on Cape Cod are aided by the reservists. Each evening the reserves conduct a water patrol in frequently used areas in coastal waters to aid any disabled small craft that might need help. These patrols many times will handle minor problems of the small boat operator before they become bigger problems for the Coast Guard units on the Cape.

Salem Air Station, Salem, Mass. This is the station when it was in operation before the rescue units were transferred to Otis A.F.B. on Cape Cod in 1970. *Photo courtesy of U.S. Coast Guard, Boston, Mass.*

Following World War II the Coast Guard began a new era in the life saving field. The helicopter was recognized early as an invaluable tool in the rescue of imperiled mariners and from the first such rescue, improvements have advanced the rotary wing aircraft to the forefront and today it is one of the primary vehicles of the modern Coast Guard.

The newest addition on Cape Cod in 1970 was the Air Station at Otis A.F.B. where the helicopters and amphibian planes operate for the entire First Coast Guard District. The operations of the air station were moved from the old bases at Salem, Mass., on the north shore and Quonset Point in Rhode Island to combine operations at a central point. All Coast Guard aviation operations are strategically located in the coastal areas of the United States in order to insure maximum protection to all of the maritime regions.

An example of the work of the helicopters at Cape Cod Station can be seen in the record for a normal week's work. The week ending August 11, 1973 involved 27 missions by helicopters, three of which were false alarms, twenty search and rescue operations and four hospital medivac cases. Two premature babies in incubators were evacuated from Cape Cod Hospital to the Boston Childrens Hospital. A helicopter flew 210 miles off shore to pick up a patient in a diabetic coma and delivered the man to a waiting ambulance at Bangor International Airport in Maine. Two other similar cases involved picking up patients off vessels at sea and delivering them to hospitals in the Boston area. The operations for this one week resulted in five lives saved and 23 persons assisted.

ABOVE: Aerial view of the entire complex at the new Coast Guard Air Station at Otis A.F.B. *Photo by Quinn.*

ABOVE: The HU-16E *ALBATROSS* amphibian plane parked on the ramp at Air Station Cape Cod. This versatile plane is used for pollution patrol and surveillance flights over the foreign fishing fleets on the Continental Shelf of the North Atlantic. BELOW: The hangar and aircraft parked on the apron at Cape Cod Air Station at Otis A.F.B. *Photos by Quinn.*

The workhorse of the service is the HH-3F, nicknamed the "Pelican". The versatility of this unique aircraft makes it indispensable in Coast Guard search and rescue operations at sea. With a 700 mile range, computerized navigation, twin turbine propulsion, the Sikorsky HH-3F added a new dimension to air-sea rescue. The photo above was made during a publicity photo mission and is not an actual rescue. *Photo by Lt. H.M. Dillian, U.S. Coast Guard.*

In addition to search and rescue duty the helicopters are called upon to help in many different types of emergencies. Aiding local law enforcement agencies, assistance in flood areas, search for drowning victims and search for lost persons in inaccessable areas are but a few of the calls answered by the modern air arm of the Coast Guard.

There is one factor today that has not changed from the old service. That is the men who fly the helicopters and planes and man the cutters and patrol boats. These men are as intrepid as their predecessors. A case in point happened in March, 1971. A distress call from

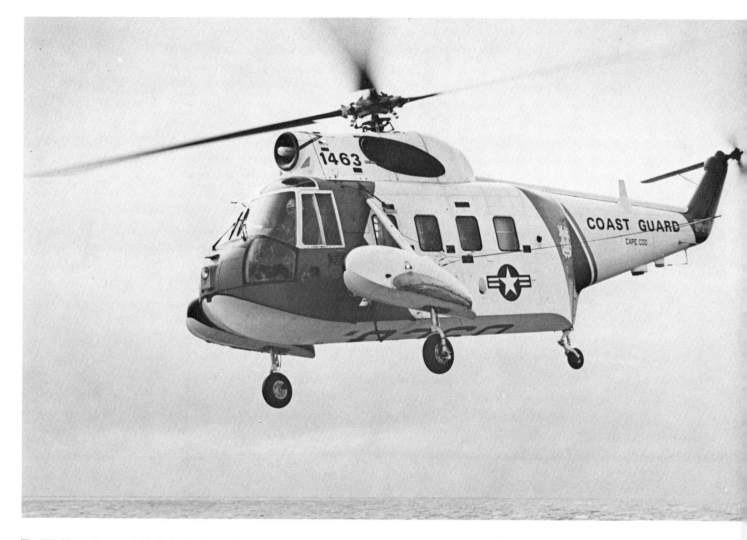

The HH-52A helicopter, dubbed the "Flying Lifeboat", used for all types of rescues and service in addition to being deployed aboard polar icebreakers. *Photo courtesy of U.S. Coast Guard, Boston, Mass.*

the fishing boat *GANNET* at almost midnight, with hurricane force winds, the vessel was sinking 68 miles southeast of Nantucket Island. A helicopter was dispatched from Air Station Cape Cod at 11:27 P.M. and when they arrived on scene, winds were 80 MPH, gusting to 90. Seas were 30 feet high and visibility was restricted in snow showers.

Conditions such as this make helicopter operations extremely hazardous but the crew gallantly battled the storm and made contact with the fishing vessel at 12:20 A.M. almost an hour after leaving the base. The high winds made transfer of the pumps impossible so the crew of the helicopter, now running low on fuel, improvised a system whereby they could trail the pumps on a 200 foot floating nylon line behind the aircraft so that the crewmen of the *GANNET* were able to pick up the line out of the water, retrieve the pumps and save their vessel.

The helicopter had to leave the scene almost as soon as they had secured the pumps aboard the stricken boat. The fuel situation aboard the helicopter was critical. It was almost 3 A.M. before the aircraft returned to the air base. The operation saved the fishing vessel *GANNET* and her six crewmen. The commander of the aircraft was subsequently awarded the Distinguished Flying Cross and the crew of the helicopter were all awarded the Air Medal. This represents but a single performance of these flying men and their amazing machines. Like the men before them, they have to go out in the worst weather. Modern innovations and electronic navigation have increased the odds in favor of the Coast Guard Aviators in their daily battles with the elements.

*EAGLE.* The age of sail is not dead. Coast Guard cadets train on this full rigged bark learning the basic fundamentals of seamanship from the deck to the end of the yardarm. A cruise aboard *EAGLE* is an unforgettable experience.

# CHAPTER 14

**The storms of the 50's and 60's strand the fishing boats,
the ships and even the Coast Guard and others.**

The *PAULMINO*, with 30,000 lbs. of haddock aboard, wrecked at Wellfleet. Constant battering by seas whipped up by 35 MPH winds caused extreme damage to the vessel and she was lost. *Photo by Quinn.*

The trawler is the mainstay of the New England fishermen. Hundreds of these craft have worked the abundant waters off Cape Cod for over two centuries. First by sail, then with engines, the vessels cast their nets from the Grand Banks of Newfoundland to the Outer Banks of North Carolina. When the fisherman leaves or returns to port, he passes Cape Cod. The pesky peninsular has wrecked many a good fishing vessel.

Early in the morning of April 3, 1959 the Boston trawler *PAULMINO* ran aground off Wellfleet in heavy rain, 35 MPH winds, and a high surf running. The boat was coming in from the fishing grounds with 30,000 pounds of haddock. She was an 83 foot trawler with a crew of seven. At 1 A.M., the Boston Coast Guard received a weak radio call for help from the vessel. The Lower Cape units of the Coast Guard were alerted and patrols along the beach were instituted by C.W.O. Leonard E. Tarvers, Group Commander, Cape Cod.

209

Thick fog and heavy seas blanketed the coast and the patrol could not spot the boat. She was on the outer bar with the seas breaking over her. The crew remained in the pilot house for five hours, waiting for help to come, but no-one knew where they were.

At dawn the Captain, Angelo Marino, directed his men to don life preservers, jump over the side and swim for the beach. At this time they were spotted by Wellfleet residents on shore and many people went to the beach to help the men out of the surf. Only four men made it ashore safely, some more dead than alive when they finally touched the beach. They were rushed to the Camp Wellfleet dispensary and given medical attention. The other three men, including the Captain, perished in the waters off Wellfleet.

The battered hull of the *PAULMINO* worked her way over the outer bar and grounded on the beach so that in the afternoon, sightseers were walking around her. The hull had been badly battered by the high seas and it was only a few days before it was completely broken up for salvage. The cargo of fish was fouled with oil and was a complete loss.

A live 60 foot finback whale grounded on the beach in Provincetown brings out a large crowd. The mammal later died and was towed out to sea by the Coast Guard. Dec. 1959. *Photo by Quinn.*

A Navy S-2F Grumman Tracker plane crashed in the ocean off Camp Wellfleet Aug. 7, 1959. The plane lost power and had to ditch in the water. One man was lost in the crash. The two pilots had to swim ashore from the plane and were helped out of the water by a local bass fisherman. *Photo by Quinn.*

In these modern times, various types of vessels wash ashore on the outer beaches of Cape Cod. On Friday, August 7, 1959 a Navy S-2F anti-submarine, hunter-killer aircraft lost power over the Atlantic and came down in the ocean 100 yards off shore in front of Camp Wellfleet. Walter F. Palmer, of Pensacola, Florida, had jumped out before the plane struck but his parachute did not open and he was killed when he hit the water.

The Pilot and co-pilot rode the plane down into the water and were injured when the plane crashed. They managed to crawl out of the wreck and swim towards shore. James Brewer of Eastham was on the beach fishing when he spotted the plane coming down. Brewer waded into the water (although he doesn't swim) and helped the two pilots out on to the beach. They were badly shaken up when they got ashore but immediate medical attention was available for them from the Army installation atop the hill behind the beach.

The plane was normally based in New Orleans, La., but was on a two week mission at Quonset Naval Air Station in Rhode Island. The plane was on a routine bombing mission over the target ship *JAMES LONGSTREET* in Cape Cod bay when it crashed. Camp Wellfleet was, at that time, an Army anti-aircraft practice base that has since closed. It is now the site of Headquarters for the Cape Cod National Seashore.

The 280 foot freighter *MONICA SMITH* of the Swedish-Chicago line lays on the sands one mile from New Beach at Provincetown. The vessel remained there for six days before she was freed by the tug *ORION. Photo by Quinn.*

It is customary on Washington's birthday weekend, for all of the automobile dealers in New England to hold open house and show off the new flivvers. But on Washington's birthday weekend in February 1960, a different type of attraction brought thousands to the Cape tip to view a shipwreck. A 280 foot freighter aground on New Beach, 1½ miles from the parking lot, coupled with sunny skies and unseasonably warm temperatures, brought the largest influx of visitors to Provincetown that had ever been recorded in the winter.

Forecasters had painted a dismal outlook for the holiday with predictions of snow, mixed with or changing to rain throughout the southeastern Massachusetts area. However, the sun shone brightly over the peninsular most of the day with some cloudiness blanketing the Cape just before sunset. On Saturday, the 21st, the Swedish freighter *MONICA SMITH*, enroute from Fall River to Halifax, Nova Scotia, was riding out gale force winds off-shore when it went aground at New Beach in Provincetown.

The *MONICA SMITH* turned out to be a mid-winter boon for Provincetown businessmen. Thousands motored down over the weekend to see the beached ship. Local merchants termed it a February tourist attraction. *Photo by Quinn.*

News of the grounding came out in all of the New England papers and on the Boston television news shows. The crowds began to arrive on Sunday morning. Provincetown is normally a quiet community at that time of the year, but by mid-day, Sunday, the town buzzed with business and excitement as two unsuccessful attempts were made, during the day, to free the beached ship.

Beach buggy service was humming with waiting lines for trips down the beach to the high and dry freighter. People by the hundreds walked the mile and a half through the soft sand from the parking lot to the beached vessel. Also benefitting from the unexpected bonanza were the eating establishments in the town, where business was termed "fabulous". Several of the eating places that remain open at that time of year were sold out during the afternoon as food supplies were rapidly consumed. Gas stations pumped thousands of gallons more than normal for an average holiday weekend and some even ran out.

Several attempts were made throughout the week to free the grounded freighter, but it wasn't until five days later that the tug *ORION,* helped by an eleven foot tide and sea anchors with the winches aboard the *SMITH*, managed to free the vessel from the sand at New Beach.

Once the sand suction was broken, the refloating task was an easy one and the ship moved out into deep water aided by the tug. The *MONICA SMITH* moved into Provincetown Harbor for inspection by officials and she got a clean bill. That afternoon the *MONICA SMITH* cleared Provincetown harbor and headed for Canada.

213

At 3 A.M., on March 6, 1960 the Coast Guard cutter *GENERAL GREENE*, stationed at Woods Hole, was sent to the aid of the tug *M. MORAN*, fighting high seas in Cape Cod Bay at the east end of the Cape Cod Canal. The *GREENE* cleared the east end of the canal and went to the tug which was anchored in gale winds and 25 to 30 foot waves. The going was very rough at the time and the wave action ripped the hawser out of the seamen's hands and it became tangled in the starboard propeller of the cutter. Commander Adrian Lonsdale ordered sea anchors put over and the high winds snapped one of the anchor chains like thread.

With only one anchor out, and that one dragging, the *GREENE* lost her starboard engine because of the fouled propeller. It now appeared that the *GREENE*, herself, needed help and the cutter *ACUSHNET* was nearby. She hurried to the assistance of the *GENERAL GREENE*. As with the tug, high seas prevented a tow line being passed and the *ACUSHNET* stayed with the *GREENE* until she started to ground on the beach and then the *ACUSHNET* had to back off. The *GENERAL GREENE* went aground at 12:10 P.M., just after noon on Spring Hill Beach in Sandwich, in a blinding snowstorm.

OPPOSITE: U.S. Coast Guard Cutter *GENERAL GREENE*. The 32 year old veteran, going to the aid of a stricken tug in Cape Cod Bay during a gale on March 6, 1960, lost an engine. With both anchors dragging she was thrown up on the beach at Spring Hill in Sandwich. ABOVE: On the day after the grounding going ashore was no problem for crewmen of the *GENERAL GREENE* as she lay on the beach. Her salvage posed a problem for the Coast Guard. *Photos by Quinn.*

The 32 year old ship was 125 feet long with a crew of 24 men. There were no injuries to the crew but the problem was how to get the ship off the beach. A huge trench was dug alongside the vessel and when the tide came in, two Army tanks were used to pull the ship into the trough. On March 9th, at 6:55 P.M., the *GENERAL GREENE* floated off the beach and back into service. She had suffered little damage in the grounding, but a few years later was retired from service. The tug *M. MORAN* managed to work her way out of trouble all by herself.

ABOVE: Salvage operations start on the beach as bulldozers dig a trough for the ship to slip into at high tide. The National Guard tanks were used to pull the ship at right angles to the beach to ease her off shore. *Aerial photo by U.S. Coast Guard.* BELOW: They had to dig a deep hole to slip the vessel into so that she could be turned around and slipped back gently into Cape Cod Bay. *Photo by U.S. Coast Guard.*

The *MARGARET ROSE* came ashore at Provincetown on Tuesday, Jan. 16, 1962. The vessel grounded south of New Beach. The Coast Guard saved seven men by breeches buoy rescue, the last time the breeches buoy was used on Cape Cod as the beach carts were retired after this wreck. *Aerial photo by U.S.Coast Guard.*

Two Gloucester draggers, the *MARGARET ROSE* and the *ANTONINO*, were fishing in Cape Cod Bay early in the morning of January 16, 1962. There was a gale blowing. Northwest winds were hitting 40 MPH when the *MARGARET ROSE*, while fishing too close to shore, struck a sand bar off New Beach, about a mile west of Wood End Lighthouse. The *ANTONINO* radioed the Coast Guard for help while a massive surf pounded over the *MARGARET ROSE* as she lay in the trough of the waves on the bar. The vessel went aground at 3:30 A.M. At 4 A.M., the Coast Guard arrived with a helicopter from Salem Air Station. The DUKWs from both the Race Point and Chatham stations were on the scene.

With a high surf running, this equipment could not rescue the men aboard the foundering dragger. Working on the rescue at this time was Bernie Webber, Boatswains Mate from the Chatham station. Webber relied on his experience and called for the breeches buoy apparatus. There was no beach cart nearby as the breeches buoy was being phased out of the service. There was apparatus at the Cape Cod Canal station, in Sandwich, and the cart was brought over the road to the scene in Provincetown.

Another angle showing the breeches buoy set-up. The Gloucester dragger, fishing inside of Race Point, was grounded by gale force winds. *Aerial photo by U.S. Coast Guard.*

Webber describes the rescue as he ran it: "At that time the Coast Guard was evaluating its rescue equipment throughout the service. Beach carts were considered to be out-moded by the service. I was one of the few that were outspoken for the retention of the apparatus, not only for the isolated circumstances where they might actually be used, but I also felt that the training the crews received from drills with these carts was invaluable in bringing men together as a team. At the time I was criticized by my superiors as old-fashioned, and a has-been.

"As if fate were to intervene, and prove me right, on 16 January, 1962 the F/V *MARGARET ROSE* grounded off-shore in heavy seas, off Race Point, with its crew in a position of peril. Attempts by amphibious DUKWs, and motor lifeboats were futile. Gathering a group of green men, and designating them positions, we rigged the breeches buoy to the *MARGARET ROSE*, and removed seven men in this way. As luck would have it, our first shot was successful."

The men were taken to the station and given first aid and released later in the day. Later that morning a short circuit developed in the pilot house of the vessel and the Coast Guard had to return to the dragger to put out a fire. This is the last recorded rescue on Cape Cod using the ancient breeches buoy apparatus. This same piece of equipment was acquired recently by the Orleans Historical Society and will be preserved for posterity. The 70 foot *MARGARET ROSE* was pulled off the beach and salvaged and went back fishing. She has since been retired.

The *GLEN & MARIA*, a New Bedford fishing dragger ashore on Nauset Beach in Chatham, October 24, 1965. The *GLEN & MARIA* came ashore at night with a green hand at the helm. The next morning the crew cooked breakfast on a driftwood fire while contemplating the results of their sloppy navigation. The Coast Guard LARC-V is parked at left. *Photo by Quinn.*

The New Bedford dragger *GLEN & MARIA* was steaming at full speed on the night of October 24, 1965 when, about midnight, she rammed into North Beach outside Chatham. Captain Wilson MacDonald of New Bedford blamed the grounding on a faulty compass.

When the 58 foot fishing vessel hit the beach, she hit with such force that it sprung the hull. The trawler was 40 years old at the time so any thoughts of salvage were given up. The boat had six tons of mixed fish aboard and this was passed out to the many sightseers from the Outer Cape that ventured down the eight miles of the outer beach in their beach buggies to see the wreck.

At dawn with the tide out, the crew was found cooking breakfast over a driftwood fire. The wreck was not moved and subsequent high surf broke up the hull and then the metal parts were salvaged off the vessel and the wooden remains of the hull were burned. There is nothing left on the beach today save a few charred logs.

ABOVE: The *GLEN & MARIA*, high and dry on the sands of Nauset Beach. The boat could not get off the beach and the pounding waves sprung all her seams and she was a total loss. Wreckers stripped her and in one week she was a charred hulk rotting in the sands. *Photo by Quinn.* BELOW: The Russians are coming . . . . . these Russian fishing vessels are anchored off Corn Hill in Truro during three weeks in September, 1964 for repairs. The smaller vessel is a repair tug, the larger vessel is one of the fleet of stern trawlers that fish on the U.S. Continental shelf from Newfoundland to the Carolina's. The larger vessel was in collision with a supply ship and had to have repairs made in calm waters. *Aerial photo by Quinn.*

A converted fishing boat engaged in coastal research hit the Chatham Bar on Sept. 1, 1967. The *FALCON* had on board about $100,000 in research gear and was conducting surveys off Nauset Beach when the grounding occurred. *Aerial photo by Quinn.*

The research vessel *FALCON*, a former New Bedford fishing dragger, came ashore on Chatham Bar on Sept. 1, 1967. The *FALCON* was engaged in coastal research when the mishap occurred and was working close to shore. The vessel had gone aground on the backside twice, earlier in the week, but managed to work her way off. However, this was the notorious Chatham Bar. An unforgiving ridge of sand that runs underwater for two miles or more off North Beach in Chatham. The bar has claimed many vessels over the years.

The Coast Guard removed the crew of seven men and during the day, efforts were made to salvage the valuable research gear aboard the sunken boat. During the afternoon, with high tides and an eight foot surf hitting the hull, any thought of floating her off was abandoned.

The *FALCON* became a menace to navigation and had to be blown up by dynamite.

The owners of the *FALCON*. Alpine Geophysical Association Inc., of Norwood, hired a local Chatham fishing boat to go out and salvage much of the electronic gear aboard. The hull had to be dynamited as it was a menace to navigation. Chatham's North Beach can be seen on the upper left of the photograph. *Aerial photo by Quinn.*

# CHAPTER 15

**Winding up a Century of Photographs of shipwrecks on outer Cape Cod.**

Storm surf at Coast Guard Beach in Eastham. Snow fences try to build up the dunes while the N.E. storms tear them down. Here you have white water for as far as the eye can see. *Photo by Quinn.*

The sea breeds the weather and the oceans of the world have a direct effect on the lives of those who live near it or on it. Thoreau said "Cape Cod is the bared and bended arm of Massachusetts" because the peninsular is shaped like an arm with a clenched fist at the end. Many of the old Cape salts claim that, when it's foggy on the Cape, a weather front moving through gets caught on that clenched fist at the end of the arm of Cape Cod and can't move out for an extra day or so and the Cape holds on to the damp weather longer than the mainland.

The simile is true but it's not usually the clenched fist at Provincetown that holds on to the weather front. Cape Cod reaches 30 miles out to sea and the temperature of the ocean usually effects the weather fronts when they get here. Sometimes they speed up and at other times they stall at the canal. Some of our summer visitors claim "it's two jackets colder on Cape Cod than in Worcester".

The dragger *DOROTHY* out of Provincetown, with Albert Silva as skipper, ran into some bad luck off the backside about 1:30 A.M. on May 9, 1973. The boat was fishing off Cahoons Hollow when it lost its electrical power and radar. She hit the sand bar, sprung a leak and was beached to prevent sinking. *Photo by Neil Nickerson, Provincetown.*

The contrast in Cape Cod weather to that on the mainland makes the Cape an ideal spot for the tourists that flock to the Cape in the summer to enjoy the many beautiful beaches. These same beaches that delight thousands of sun lovers in the summer are the sites of the ship disasters in the winter.

It is impossible to determine the exact number of wrecks that have occurred around Cod since the Pilgrims first landed here, however, it is safe to say that the number exceeds, without exaggeration, 5,000, given the factual information gathered from the available records.

In all probability, more than half of this number were wrecks of minor importance. Ships that became lost in the fog and had gone aground without mortal damage to hull and rigging. Not all storms are killers and many ships that are driven ashore were able, on the next high tide, to kedge off the sands and resume their journey. A calm sea will lap gently at the sides of a vessel aground and cause little or no damage.

The ships that were totally wrecked became fodder for the wreckers of the Cape and many were burned to get rid of them while others were ripped apart for lumber and firewood. Many Cape Cod cottages are supported by oak foundations that were steeped in brine and which will defy the ages.

Most of the vessels that lie buried in the sands of the Cape are out below the low water mark. The endless erosive action of the Atlantic Ocean eats away at the backside of Cape Cod and vessels that are high and dry today are awash in the surf tomorrow and end up as waterlogged hulks that loom out at low tide with grotesque shapes and forms.

224

Efforts to save the *DOROTHY* were fruitless. After two days work, the surf kept banging at her and started to wreck her. Crewmen removed the salvageable gear aboard, and she started to go the way of most beached boats on the backside. *Photo by Neil Nickerson, Provincetown.*

At 1 A.M., on May 9, 1973, a Provincetown boat named *DOROTHY* was fishing off the backside near Cahoon's Hollow in Wellfleet. There used to be a Life Saving/Coast Guard station at Cahoon's Hollow but it was closed and is now a night club for summer visitors of Wellfleet.

The *DOROTHY* lost all her power suddenly, shortly after 1 A.M., and was plunged into darkness. The vessel got caught up in a few waves and ended up on the bar just off the beach right in front of the old Cahoon's Hollow station.

For two days her crew and many other people worked against time and tide and the incessant surf to try to save the *DOROTHY*, but fate was against them. The *DOROTHY* came ashore on Wednesday, May 9th and on Friday, May 11th, a front end loader machine broke into the hull to retrieve the engine. On Saturday, the wreckage from the vessel was strewn up and down the beach for half a mile.

ABOVE: The wave action has started to spell the end of the *DOROTHY*. Wreckage is strewn along the beach and the waves hack away at the hull in its exposed location. *Photo by Quinn.* BELOW: Four days after grounding all that is left on the beach is splintered wreckage and firewood. *Photo by William P. Quinn, Jr.*

TOP: Wreckage of an old tugboat on the bayside shore at Eastham. ABOVE: Wreckage from ships and boats is spread up and down the whole length of Cape Cod. This shot was made in Provincetown out on Long Point. A beach taxi has stopped to give tourists a look at an authentic shipwreck. Probably an old fishing boat that outlived its usefulness and was beached and later burned for a bonfire by beach party goers. RIGHT: The ocean acts as a huge hydraulic dredge, moving sand around, covering and sometimes uncovering wrecks. These ribs of a sunken vessel were visible in 1962 but have since disappeared. *Photos by Quinn.*

Not all of the shipwrecks around Cape Cod have disappeared. There is much to see today. While most of the wreckage is visible only to skin divers under water, there are wrecks visible in many areas on the backside.

In Provincetown on Peaked Hill Bars the remains of the British Frigate *SOMERSET* are sometimes visible at low tide two miles east of the Race Point Coast Guard Station. In North Truro, at Head of the Meadow Beach, the Hamburg bark *FRANCES* is out of the water at low tide, a short walk from the parking lot. Many Cape Codders have pieces of wreckage that they haul off the beach and hang on the wall of a den or playroom and label it with data and photographs.

TOP: The *MONTCLAIR* wreckage 30 years later, March 4, 1957 on Nauset Beach, Orleans. Mid-hull section. ABOVE: Another aerial photograph of the wreck of the *PENDLETON* taken in the summer of 1972, twenty years after that fateful night when the tanker broke in half in a storm six miles off Chatham. *Photos by Quinn.*

In Orleans, almost buried in the dunes of Nauset is a section of the hull of the *MONT CLAIR*. A beach vehicle is needed to view her. The easiest to view is the stern section of the tanker *PENDLETON* which lies east of Monomoy Island and is clearly visible with binoculars from in front of the Chatham Coast Guard Station at the parking lot.

# THE TARGET SHIP

The largest wreckage in view is not from a Cape Cod shipwreck but the ship itself which was moved to her present position on purpose. The best description of the *JAMES LONG-STREET* is that it looks like steel plated swiss cheese. Since 1944 the ship has withstood bombs, rockets, missiles and explosions fore and aft by units of the Navy, Air Force and National Guard bomber and fighter planes.

The history of the ship is not an epic saga of the sea. She was built and launched in the 1940's, one of the hundreds of Liberty ships that helped win the war for Uncle Sam. They were more affectionately known to her crews as Kaiser's Coffins, named after the original builder, Henry J. Kaiser.

The *JAMES LONGSTREET* made a few voyages overseas as a cargo ship and was accidently grounded in a storm. Damaged beyond economic repair, she was towed, full of barrels for buoyancy, to the spot in Cape Cod Bay she now occupies. There, she was set up as a target ship for most of the surrounding military aerial hardware in the New England area.

The ship lies two miles west of the Eastham shore and is clearly visible from shore. In the summertime, the aerial fireworks provide daily and evening entertainment for the tourists that turn out along the bay shores from Dennis to Wellfleet.

The attacks on the ship are made in all weather and at most anytime of the day or night up until 10 P.M., during the summer time. Some of the early morning flights are referred to as the dawn patrol, after an old Errol Flynn movie. The area around the ship is listed on marine charts as a restricted area because of the varying amounts of unexploded ordinance lying on the bottom near the ship.

The *JAMES LONGSTREET*, a battered old Liberty Ship, was grounded in the middle of Cape Cod Bay in 1944 for use as a target ship for the many different flying services in the area. The Navy, National Guard and Air Force have all had a part in the destruction of this derelict. *Photo by Quinn.*

ABOVE: The top deck of the *JAMES LONGSTREET* looks like the blitz. Bomb tails litter the deck and the rocket holes make the whole vessel look like swiss cheese. A stroll along the deck will give one an eerie feeling almost like a haunted house. *Photo by Quinn.*

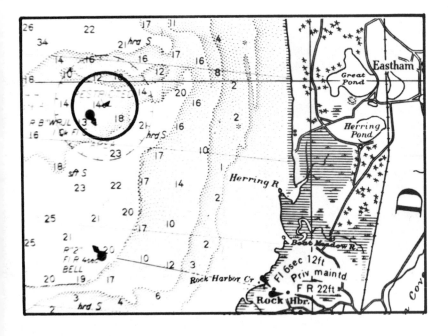

The remains of the *JAMES LONGSTREET* lay in Cape Cod Bay off Eastham. Chart 1208 shows the area to be restricted.

Aboard the ship itself, it's like another world. The utter destruction resembles war torn Europe before it was reconstructed. There are small and large bomb holes, pieces of bombs lying around on deck and lots of rust. Local natives say that it's the rust that is holding the ship together. For the ship to have survived almost 30 years of bombardment, even the small target bombs, is some kind of tribute to the durability of American shipbuilding during the war. A visit to the ship is an unforgettable experience, and illegal, as no one is supposed to go aboard.

LEFT: The winter of 1970-71 was long and cold with much ice and took its toll on many of the smaller boats in the Cape harbors. In Provincetown three fishing boats were wrecked. This is the *REVENGE*, battered against a pier until it split open. ABOVE: At McMillan Wharf, *JIM'S BOAT* was wrecked by the wave action against the side of the grounded boat. *Photos by Quinn.*

BELOW RIGHT: A victim of the "70-71" winter was the *WALLACE & ROY* which broke her mooring and ended up wrecked on the Provincetown Breakwater at the west end of the harbor. The boat was damaged extensively below the waterline and salvage was not possible. BELOW: In Hyannis Harbor the fishing dragger *PAULINE BERTHA* split a seam while trying to fight the ice in Lewis Bay and went to the bottom in the middle of Hyannis Harbor. *Photos by Quinn.*

The schooner *CHATANOOGA* ashore on Nauset Beach, Orleans, December 12, 1890. The *CHATANOOGA*, 156 tons, out of Bucksport, Me. with Capt. Morgan, was bound from New York City to Bucksport with a cargo of coal, and a crew of four. The schooner was a total loss. She stranded 500 yds. south of the Orleans Life Saving Station. *Photo by H. K. Cummings, Orleans.*

The American schooner *JOHN ROMMELL, JR.* badly iced up, ashore in Provincetown during a storm in February 1875. The ship was a total loss. *Photo courtesy of Cape Cod Photos - Orleans, Mass.*

234

Cape Codders decorate the gable end of their cottages
with the Quarterboards from wrecked ships. There are
some familiar names among the houses in Chatham
at the elbow of the Cape. *Photos by Quinn.*

# EPILOGUE

Since time began and man first ventured forth upon the sea to find new worlds, there has not been enough time to learn the secrets of the seas. In his quest for perfection, man will overlook the ambiguity of the sea. He can build the finest ship afloat, and, in the course of nature, watch the sea destroy what he has built.

On the backside of Cape Cod, the Mooncussers, the Wreckers and Rum Runners have given up the ghost to practice more lucrative pursuits as lawyers, real estate brokers and motel operators carrying on honest trade with the summer tourists.

The shipwrecks will no doubt continue on the Cape, as will the fog and storms. The square riggers and schooners have disappeared now, but have not been forgotten. The bleached bones of once proud ships still serve as anonymous tombstones to the vessels whose names are written on the sandy shores that wrecked them. In the quaint little towns, Cape Cod cottages are trimmed with their quarterboards, their names emblazoned in gold leaf. The list is long and tragic, some of their names are legends: The *NORTHERN LIGHT*, The *MORNING STAR*, *WINGED ARROW* and *LADY OF THE OCEAN*. *LADY FRANK-LIN*, *LORNA DOONE*, *ETHEL SWIFT* and *LITTLE LOTTIE*. The *NAUTILUS*, *NEPTUNE*, *VENUS* and *TRIMPH*. Their Captains' names are etched in granite in the grave-yards of the Lower Cape. They built a wall of shipwrecks stretching from Monomoy to Provincetown as a monument to the intrepid men who sailed them. The hulls lie interred in the sands, never again to feel the spread of canvas on the bare poles and spars that now lie rotting in the surf wash.

As the night brightens into dawn and the lighthouses dim their flashing beacons, another day will bring new ships to sea, to pass Cape Cod and salute those who have passed these shores before.

THE END.

From Monomoy to Race Point, the sun bleached bones jut out of the sands. About every mile on the backside is some wreckage, small or large. These are in Chatham on North Beach and in the background, that small dot on the horizon is the remains of the wreck of the *PENDLETON* off Monomoy Island. *Photo by Quinn.*

236

# ACKNOWLEDGEMENTS

The search for the photographs in this book extended from North Carolina up the east coast to the state of Maine. About one third of the photographs were borrowed, copied and then returned. Some were purchased. A grateful "Thank You" is extended to all those who loaned photographs and others who aided me in the research of information.

The collection of old photographs began in the 1950's with the loan of the glass plates of the late Henry K. Cummings of Orleans and thanks go to the Trustees of the Snow Library in Orleans. Appreciation is extended to other friends; John Schramm and the late Harold Cooper of Cape Cod Photos in Orleans for the Rosenthal collection of pictures from the lower Cape area; to Paul C. Morris of Nantucket for part of his large collection; Chad Smith of the Peabody Museum in Salem, Massachusetts; Dick Kelsey of Chatham; Lt. H. M. Dillian, PIO at Air Station, Cape Cod, U.S.C.G. and the First Coast Guard District Information Office, Boston; Ed Lohr and other personnel of the Cape Cod National Seashore and Gordon Caldwell of Hyannis, staff photographer at the Cape Cod Standard Times, and to the many others whose names appear in the credit lines of the photographs.

Additional thanks are extended to the Cape Codder newspaper and Editor Mal Hobbs for the piece on Mooncussing; to Sumner Towne, Editor of the Cape Cod Independent newspaper; to Ben Harrison of Buzzards Bay for his photographs and history of the Cape Cod Canal and to my brother Howard W. Quinn for the exciting tale of the wreck of the *MONTCLAIR*.

Again, deep gratitude to all those who helped me in the acquisition of this material.

W.P.Q.

The two masted lumber schooner *WILLIAM BOARDMAN* ashore at Eastham, June 13, 1891. This unlucky schooner was refloated and completed her journey to New York, but when she returned, bound for Scituate, Mass. with a cargo of coal, she ran afoul of the Chatham Bars and was a total loss. The crew of four were saved however. *Photo by H. K. Cummings, Orleans.*

The Island Steamer *SANKATY* ran on the rocks off Wilburs Point in Buzzards Bay on February 20, 1917. She was steaming towards New Bedford in a dense fog when the accident happened. She suffered damage to her plates and was not back in service until March 30th. *Photo courtesy of Peabody Museum of Salem.*

# BIBLIOGRAPHY

## Books

Provincetown by Herman A. Jennings—1890
Shipwrecks on Cape Cod by Isaac M. Small—1928
Mooncussers of Cape Cod by Kittredge
The Outermost House by Beston—1928
Disaster on Devil's Bridge by Hough—1963
Nauset on Cape Cod, A History of Eastham by Lowe—1968
Cape Cod, Its People and their History by
      Kittredge—1930
American Sailing Coasters of the North Atlantic
      by Morris—1973
Bradfords History
Life Library of Photography
U.S. Coast Guard History
Deyo's History of Barnstable County—1890
Life Saving Nantucket by Stackpole—1972
Wrecks Around Nantucket by Gardner—1915

## Periodicals

U.S. Life Saving Service Annual Reports: 1884, 1886,
      1888, 1889, 1890, 1891, 1893, 1894, 1895, 1896,
      1897, 1898, 1899, 1902, 1905, 1908, 1909, 1913,
      1914.
U.S. Coast Guard Annual Reports: 1922, 1924.
U.S. Corps of Engineers reports-Cape Cod Canal, The
New York Maritime Register.

## Newspapers

The Provincetown Advocate, The Cape Codder, The
      Vineyard Gazette, The Falmouth Enterprise, The
      New Bedford Daily Mercury, The New Bedford
      Standard Times, The Cape Cod Standard Times,
      The Boston Globe, The Boston Post, The Wareham
      Courier, The Lower Cape Chronicle.

## Personal Correspondence & Interviews

Ministry of Defence, Naval Historical Library, London
      England.
National Maritime Museum, London England.
Historian Edison P. Lohr, Cape Cod National Seashore
Albert E. Snow, Orleans, Mass.
Henry Beetle Hough, Edgartown, Mass.
Capt. Nathan L. Baggs, Nova Scotia
Yngve Rongner, Eastham, Mass.
Ben Harrison, Buzzards Bay, Mass.
Lt. H.M. Dillian, U.S. Coast Guard

## Museums

Peabody Museum of Salem, Mass.
Bureau of National Archives, Washington, D.C.

Photos taken in June 1969 of breeches buoy drill at Sandwich Coast Guard Station on the Cape Cod Canal at Sandwich, Mass. This is one of the last drills as soon after this the beach cart apparatus was retired from the Coast Guard Service. *Photos by Howard Quinn.*